THE ARTIST'S GUIDE TO HIS MARKET

THE
ARTIST'S
GUIDE TO HIS
MARKET

BY BETTY CHAMBERLAIN

WATSON-GUPTILL PUBLICATIONS, NEW YORK

In memory of
Just Lunning and Ben Shahn

Contents

Introduction

If you are a fine artist, how can you find a place to exhibit your work? This is a universal question. As one painter has summed it up: "The greatest problem which professional painters and sculptors have is that of finding exhibition space. Where to show his work? This is becoming increasingly difficult. The galleries have a full roster of artists; there are few co-operatives, juried shows which are limited in size, too few art associations—in short, fine artists face the discouraging situation of being unable to find places to exhibit."

The mental and psychological strain of the situation is manifest in a recent comment by a New York artist: "I have spent years cultivating the aesthetic sensibilities only to have run dry of the stuff that makes artists known. I cannot paint pictures and have the pictures stack up in my apartment. All the worthwhile effort is wasted. Negative feelings arise, and many questions are raised as to why I paint with such fervor. . ."

And a leading New York dealer just wrote me saying: "From my observation I would say there are as many good artists not in galleries as there are those who have galleries."

These problems are certainly very real indeed and have been growing steadily; for despite the increase in the numbers of galleries, the number of serious artists has grown much more. This book aims to provide information of a practical nature to artists who are seeking to overcome these difficulties of exposure and sale of their work. It supplies information about dealers and their practices, derived from art galleries large and small, in New York and elsewhere, as background material to help guide the artist. The dealer in business, and those who plan to go into the business, may well find this information useful as a yardstick for accepted practices.

Art Information Center

Most of the information given here is derived from years of experience with thousands of artists and hundreds of dealers. Very little has been published on this subject. In 1959, the author established the Art Information Center, Inc., in New York City, a non-profit, tax-deductible organization (the only one of its kind so far). The Board of Directors is composed of the following, in alphabetical order: Betty Chamberlain, Stanley William Hayter, Jacob Lawrence, Just Lunning (*dec.*), Joseph B. Martinson, Ben Shahn (*dec.*). The information in the book is largely based on the work of the Center. The purpose of this office is to give free assistance to artists who wish to find outlets for their work, and to dealers who seek new talent. It also helps curators, collectors, the art press, and the general public to locate the work of any living artist.

The Center came into being as a result of eighteen years of experience in museum work, during which it became apparent to me that museums were unable to supply much help in these directions, although there were ever-increasing needs. The number of artists and galleries both mushroomed after World War II to the point where neither artist nor dealer could keep up with the growth, nor could they have any over-all perspective on the art scene. Thus the artist was at a loss to know where to try to show his work, and the dealer did not know how to help him. Confusion, disappointment, and discouragement resulted. Moreover, no one knew how to find out where to see or buy work by the thousands of living artists who *did* have gallery affiliations, for there was no source of information on what gallery handled which artists.

Services to artists

The Art Information Center, Inc., was therefore set up as a clearing house of information in these areas of contemporary fine arts. It asks no fee or commission of anyone at any time. It sees by appointment some 500 artists per year and, on the basis of slides of paintings or photographs of sculpture brought by the artist, it suggests some galleries most likely to be interested in the particular kind of work. These recommendations are also made partly on the basis of knowledge as to which galleries are more apt to be able to take new work. For many dealers have a full roster and see no point in wasting everyone's time by looking at any more work. Indeed, most New York galleries refer artists to the Center when the artists just walk in at random. The dealers are glad to be able to give the artists some directions; many an artist has learned in this way about the Center's services.

Needless to say, in order to know what kind of work the galleries are handling and what their situation is, it is necessary for me to go to visit many every week. For verbal descriptions without the visual actuality tend to be meaningless—works of art are not easily categorized. Nor are "directions" of galleries. If they were, if the whole feeling of the contemporary art field could be computerized, then IBM could do the job. But I have seen too many hundreds of artists who have had to gird their loins even to come to the Center, and who dread facing a dealer. To subject them to computerizing, to hand them a "canned" list, would be a most discouraging brush-off just when they need that least.

All artists who come by appointment are invited to call the Center if, in going to galleries, any questions arise in their minds about terms proposed or if there is anything else on which they would like to consult. The Center encourages artists to report any questionable procedures which they may encounter among galleries they approach, for in this way I am better able to help the next artists who come to the Center. It is impossible to tell by the looks or the location of a gallery whether or not its operation is conducted on a professional basis. Sometimes artists deviate from the list given them and wander in to see a dealer who welcomes them warmly, enthuses over their impressive talents, offers a one-man show. Usually these are non-professional galleries, and if the artists phone the Center, they are always so advised frankly. For affiliation with such galleries would not only cost the professional artist undue sums of money, but could also hurt his professional reputation. There is nothing illegal about such galleries, and perhaps they serve a purpose for amateurs. But when the Center learns of instances of complete misrepresentation on the part of any gallery, this is reported to the Better Business Bureau, the Art Dealers' Association, and the State Attorney General's Office.

The time it takes to see each artist, to study his slides concentratedly, to select about ten or twelve suggested galleries for him from a list of some 400 New York galleries—plus inevitable incoming phone interruptions—runs from about forty minutes to an hour. This is often hard for artists, seeking immediate appointments, to understand; they wonder why they can't just drop in for five minutes. In addition to compiling a selective list of galleries for each artist, the Center gives each artist some information on practices and procedures, appropriate approaches to dealers, business terms to seek, what to look for, and what to look *out* for in outlets for display.

But obviously this personal service must be limited. There are so many artists who are too far away to visit the Center. The following chapters aim to disseminate such information not only much more widely, but in more complete detail than is possible in appointment periods. Even if you can visit the Center for individual help, you should derive from these pages much supplementary information which is equally important. And if you cannot make a personal appointment, there are many suggestions here on how to determine your own best procedures.

Services to dealers

Each artist who communicates with the Center is invited to leave or send in duplicate slides or photographs, so that dealers who come in, seeking new talent, may select from these reproductions any artist whose work is of interest to them.

All reproductions left at or sent to the Center should be labeled with the dimensions of the originals, the medium, and the artist's name. Size is often important to galleries, and it is impossible to determine it from a tiny reproduction; medium can be confusing also in reproduction; name is essential on each slide because dealers inevitably mix up the slides they have viewed, and then no one can know where they really belong.

An interested dealer then gets in touch directly with the artist, usually arranging to visit his studio to see originals. Occasionally, when geographical distance is a problem, the dealer may ask the artist to send a few works. There are usually some 500 to 700 unaffiliated artists represented in this record of reproductions at the Center—a file which, of course, changes constantly as some artists find gallery affiliations and are removed, and new artists are added.

Many dealers, both in and outside of New York, have obtained their artists in this way when they were about to open galleries. Frequently, dealers come from far-flung areas, seeking to represent and show in their regions some interesting new artists from "the effete East," or from "the art center of the world." Naturally, dealers prefer to select an artist who does not have a contract with another gallery, for this would require them to split commissions with the other dealers. In some cases, the Center receives a written description of the kind of work desired by a dealer who is far from New York; the Center then selects some reproductions to send on a short loan.

Services to museums, collectors, art press, general public

The Center keeps up-to-date records of living artists who have gallery affiliations, and anyone may call or write to locate their work. At last count there have been over 19,000 living artists listed, with their gallery affiliations, since the Center was founded in 1959. In order to maintain this record accurately, a form is sent each September to all New York galleries and to a great many others in cities throughout the U.S. and abroad, on which the galleries list the artists they represent and handle. Because artists frequently change their gallery affiliations, the records must be checked and changed at the beginning of each season (the art season in New York is roughly from late September to June 1), because there are so many changes from one seasonal contract year to the next. In addition, the Center is on a great many mailing lists, and all information is regularly listed from brochures and announcements. All listings from major art publications, art columns, and advertisements are also checked regularly.

It should be stressed that this information aims to apply only to the fine arts. The Center does not work in the field of illustration or commercial art. And naive purchasers who buy in some out-of-the-way shop, after a sales talk about how "famous" the artist is, may be doomed to disappointment when they call the Center, only to find that the artist is not listed because he has never shown in any recognized gallery. Of course, no listing is complete. But if an artist is not listed in the Center's files, two other compilations are always consulted: *Who's Who in American Art* and *The International Directory of Arts.*

Hundreds of calls and letters, seeking this service, come into the Center; no record of how many is kept, for the Center is too busy answering them. Museums are anxiously looking for a particular artist's work to fill out a planned show. The Internal Revenue Service wants to know all galleries who have ever represented certain artists in order to obtain three appraisals each on works of art to be given to public institutions as tax-deductible gifts (some donors try to get away with a tax deduction of several times the value of the donation). An art writer or reviewer needs to check on work by a particular artist. A businessman wants to buy paintings by certain artists for his offices. A housewife has seen a sculpture in a friend's garden and wants to buy a similar one by the same artist. A tourist is particularly anxious, while in New York, to see work by so-and-so. There are even, from time to time, inquiries for the purpose of settling a bet or solving a crossword puzzle.

Collectors sometimes call anxiously for an artist's home address, but this is never revealed by the Center unless the artist has no gallery affiliation. For too often their purpose is to bypass the gallery commission and try to talk the artist into selling at lower prices.

Other services

The Center never attempts to duplicate any information service which is available elsewhere. If people inquire for artists' biographies, they are referred to their galleries. If they are looking for grants and fellowships, they are sent to the Foundation Library Center in New York. If they want to enter competitive shows, they are told which publications list them. If they need to refer to critical reviews, they are referred to the *Art Index* in the public library. If they want to know what museums and art schools exist in any part of the country, they are referred to the *American Art Directory.* The Center tries only to fill gaps where the information does not exist anywhere else, and to direct and guide people to other sources of information which do exist. It does try to know about where you can take special courses, like Chinese brushwork or welded sculpture; about where you can go to work from a model in the evening; about where to apply to get space in the Washington Square outdoor shows.

1

Are you ready to exhibit?

How can you know whether you are professional in your work, still a student, or really an amateur? In extreme cases, doting mamas sometimes try to push their teen-age darlings into gallery shows because their high school art teachers graded them well after their first year or two and mentioned the word "talent." Obviously, the serious-minded artist knows that the urge and the realization must come from within, not from goading or flattery by relatives and friends. It is an old dictum that no one should try to become a fine artist unless he has to, when the inner drive is too strong to overcome. For the pursuit of art as a career is generally not only unremunerative, but costly; the competition is fierce; and real recognition is achieved by only a small percentage.

A naive but direct inquiry about this dilemma came to me from North Dakota: "Will you please send me information on how to become an 'established painter'? What is the process by which one is established? Also how to judge between using another picture for reference, and plagiarism?"

Some questions to ask yourself

Perhaps it will help you to ask yourself some questions:

(1) Do you work on a steady, regular basis, or are you "spotty" and interrupted in your output? Some artists work very slowly. Peter Blume, for example, may spend twelve years on one painting and all its preliminary drawings and sketches. But such artists nevertheless work regularly and consistently, not on an "I must wait for the mood" basis.

(2) Do you differentiate between your better and your less successful work? Do you "sleep on it" to get perspective so you can judge what to keep and what to discard? This is important not only for future exhibition purposes, but also for your own development and for where you place emphasis and direction. I was gratified indeed when I received an unusual note from a New York artist: "Kindly cancel my appointment; I will contact you later. I have come to the realization that the work I have been doing is not up to what I want to do." For it is only this kind of self-realization that is of value; no one else can do that for you.

(3) Is your style consistent? True, many artists work in more than one style at the same time. But usually, in the case of an artist who has "jelled," there is a strong vein of similarity, unity, and consistency, even between two fairly different styles. Or the artist, on self-examination, realizes that he is really leaning more towards one of his directions, sometimes using others for experimentation, practice, breadth of development—as studies for an ultimate production. If you go in too many different directions at once, you may well spread too thin in all of them.

A Singaporean Chinese girl wrote, wanting to come to the U.S.: "I am artistically inclined, but I feel frustrated here . . . my artistic talents are just not exploited. What I would like to do: architecture, pottery, ceramics, fashion designing, stage designing, sculpture, portrait and fig-

17

ure drawing in all media, and abstract art." You have to admire the ambition of such a project!

If you are still trying out numerous approaches and are not sure what really speaks for you, then perhaps you are not ready to show.

(4) Do you have a sufficient body of consistent work to show? Dealers generally want to see some fifteen or twenty, recently executed by the artist, before deciding whether or not to show him. They are not interested in work done earlier in a different style until you become old and famous, like Picasso, and warrant a retrospective exhibition showing development in various periods. They want work in your current style, which is likely to continue to come out of your studio for at least some months ahead. What to do with a body of work in a previous style? Forget it. Perhaps put some of the best away for your future perusal of your development; perhaps give some as a present to your mother-in-law.

(5) Do you try to be "in the swing" of new movements? If you are concerned with bandwagons and bend your talents towards adjusting to the latest fashion, the chances are that your work will not hold up over any length of time. There is always room somewhere for truly creative, original, and talented work in any style, even if it may seem "old fashioned." The faddist, on the other hand, though he may make a momentary coup, is all too likely to wind up as an opportunistic flash in the pan, usually smacking of imitation and derivation.

An artist, faced with this problem of change in what is "avant-garde" in Europe, wrote from Munich: "Excuse me, that you receive herewith a letter from an unknown person. But I heard you can help painters to get an exhibition in N.Y. More I don't know. I made already exhibit in Paris, but in Paris it is very difficult since 2 years with the abstract paintings. I like to exhibit my abstract aquarelles next year. Should I show perhaps with figuratives and flowers?"

If the work is not really yours, emanating from your own basic need to express it your own way, better not do it. Or if you do it just to prove to yourself that you can, don't show it.

(6) Do you expect to make a living from your art alone? Even those artists who do have reputable galleries representing them run into difficulties.

John Canaday of *The New York Times*, who writes periodically on the plight and problems of the artist, described one, "typical of many, whose increasing reputation, after exhibitions of his work in a series of major shows, is not reflected in increasing income."

He also reported on the experiences of another artist who, he says, faces "a problem faced by all artists, that of exhibition in a New York gallery." This artist, who has had eight New York shows in the past sixteen years, "must seem to most artists to have achieved more than average success," says Mr. Canaday. "His gallery is an old, well established one, not particularly aggressive but much respected—dependable and financially stable." But "expense is certain and profit is at least uncertain from a gallery show," and Mr. Canaday goes on to quote the experiences of this seemingly fortunate artist: after paying the required costs of framing and publicity for his latest one-man show and selling ten paintings from the show, he cleared a total of $470 "to cover the cost of paints, canvas, and studio space for the two years' work represented by the exhibition. . . . The gallery's side of the story is that it took in about $325 a week to cover expenses during the three weeks of the show. This is obviously much less than it costs to run the place."

The artist told Mr. Canaday: "There is no asset for the average artist like the socially gifted wife. From all of this, it is pretty apparent that I have exactly three choices. I can find myself such a wife, or I can kill myself, or I can continue to support myself by teaching, which I am quite happily committed to doing." [Short quotes from John Canaday © 1968 by *The New York Times* Company. Reprinted by permission.]

Only a handful of top-name artists are able to live by their creations; indeed many who are well known still must do something else for livelihood. There is an informative discussion of this problem—and of some of the other ways in which artists make a living—in the book, *Art Career Guide* by Donald Holden (Watson-Guptill Publications, New York, 1967, pp. 69-71). It is unrealistic, wishful thinking on the part of any fine artist to believe that he is going to earn his living by his works of art. Should it happen in the course of time, it will be a great bonanza—but don't count on it.

Earning a living

Better to try to figure out a job for yourself which permits you as much time as possible for your art. Some artists prefer related work, like teaching or commercial art; others prefer a complete divorce between their money-making and their chosen profession. Some are able to work remuneratively at engineering drafting or an applied art, producing an income in only three to six months sufficient to leave them completely free for their own work the rest of the year. Many work full-time, regular job hours, and still have the drive for a large art output in their spare time. One of the most idyllic artist-jobs I have heard of was that of a Northwest artist who sat painting for many seasons in a forest fire tower north of Seattle, paid to keep an eye out for smoke.

Museum jobs

If you seek employment in a museum, there is usually not much value in going to an employment agency; go, rather, to the personnel departments of the museums themselves. Even dealer galleries very rarely turn to any employment agency when they need assistants; they are more apt to use the grapevine method. For professional jobs in museums, the American Association of Museums in Washington publishes openings throughout the U.S. in its monthly *Museum News,* and in the middle of each month a supplemental *Professional Placement Bulletin.* These are available in most art libraries, or by a $15 membership in the association, open to anyone.

Teaching jobs

For teaching jobs, there are placement bureaus in the colleges and universities, and the College Art Association of America maintains a placement bureau for its members ($15 per year). Such teaching positions usually require a degree in education or some other graduate degree. Those independent art schools which do not give degrees will much more readily employ artist-teachers who do not have degrees. Some of these schools will employ artists only on a part-time basis, for they feel that it is important for the artist to have sufficient time to continue his own work in his studio. Many have evening courses.

Some artists have found employment in various fields through the U.S. Employment Service or through state employment agencies.

2

Galleries
and how
they function

Fine arts galleries deal primarily in paintings, sculpture, mixed media, graphics. [Note: The publishers make a distinction in the use of the words *mediums* and *media*. *Media* refers to the technical materials with which the artist is working. *Mediums* signifies the concoction an artist adds to his paint to change its viscosity or texture.]

"Art dealers" versus "picture dealers"

The Art Dealers' Association of America, to which about 100 older, established galleries belong, makes the distinction between a true "art dealer" and a dealer in "pictures." The dealer in "pictures," says the Association, is engaged in "an entirely honorable business, but essentially different from the fine art business." Thus the artist who wrote me from Holland was, from his discription, seeking a "picture" dealer: "I am a painter of old dutch paintings, and should like to come in contact with a person who is buying art paintings, so my question is, if you can give me those addresses." The Art Information Center, however, functions only in the fine arts field of "art dealers."

The Art Dealers' Association defines the true "art dealer" as one who "is making a substantial contribution to the cultural life of his community by the nature of the works offered for sale, worthwhile exhibitions, and informative catalogs or other publications. Art dealers in the leading art centers—both members and non-members of the association—perform a most important function. It is the dealers rather than the museums which first discover and exhibit the works of new artists. [Note : Exceptions to this statement surely should be made in cases such as Alfred H. Barr, Jr., first Director of New York's Museum of Modern Art.] The dealers' exhibitions, which are open to the public without charge, are among the most important 'free shows' of any kind thus available. They are an outstanding benefit to artists, museums, collectors, and the public generally."

A legal case, based on this assumption of benefit, was won a number of years ago by the Leo Castelli Gallery in New York. Neighbors protested that his gallery violated a zoning law: his gallery was a few feet beyond the prescribed commercial area. However, he proved to the court that he was acting much more as an educational center than as a commercial one: his door was always open, free to all; his carpets were worn out by students and scholars who never bought; his publications were sent free to libraries and universities. The final result was that he was allowed to remain in the same location.

But, on the other hand, the association warns that "art dealers are engaged in business. They hope to operate at a profit. . . . Their galleries are not museums. Their owners and operators are primarily engaged in buying and selling works of art." They go on to warn: "Dealers' galleries are not public service stations and they do not offer to the public drinking water, telephones, or toilets."

Indeed it is well to keep this in mind. I went with a visiting out-of-town artist to a gallery preview, and as soon as she reached the crowded party, she made a beeline for the gallery's telephone. Fortunately, I was able to distract her and explain that this would not be appreciated. "But it's only a local call," she said, accustomed to unlimited calls in her home town. But aside from the cost of every local call in New York—and why should a dealer pay for all visitors' calls? —the gallery does not want its line tied up so no one can reach it.

The Art Dealers' Association of America is a non-profit organization of dealers in New York and elsewhere in the United States, who are elected to membership on the basis of belief in the dealer's knowledge of his particular field and in his complete integrity. The association is active in combating fraudulent practices. A prospective member must have been in business for at least five years, must have a good reputation for honesty in his dealings, and must be considered by the association a true "art dealer." The requirement for ethical standards applies not only to dealings with the public, but also with artists. Any dealer who is a member of the association will doubtless have its booklet describing its activities and listing all its members, who are generally considered the "cream of the crop" among art galleries. So unless you have already gained a considerable reputation, it is not very likely that you can start out in one of these galleries. But the standards they set are practiced by many galleries which are not members. These standards, which are described in greater detail below, are most helpful to the artist.

Some standards to look for

The "professional" gallery charges a commission on sales, but does not require any fees from the artist. This kind of dealer makes his living from sales, not from the artist's pocket. The costs charged to the artist by a "professional" dealer are the actual out-of-pocket costs for publicity for a one-man show, and he is willing to show you the bills for these costs.

If he publicizes a group show, that is *his* financial responsibility, not yours. If there are shipping costs, he may expect you to pay these at least one way. If you are a painter, he will expect you to deliver your work already framed. If you want total coverage in insurance, you may have to supplement his insurance, for almost no dealer carries insurance for 100% of value. These are the terms to look for, based on the concept that the dealer should be in business because he has judgment both for quality and for what will sell.

What to look out for

The "non-professional" dealer, of which there are many, may insist on a guarantee against commissions—which means that you assure him of anything from $150 to $2,500 in sales commissions, whether he sells that much or not! Naturally, this removes his incentive for making sales, for he knows that you will have to pay him anyway. And remember that for every $1,000 guarantee you give him, he would have to sell $2,500 worth of your work for him to get the usual 40% commission and for you to get back your $1,000.

He may also charge hanging fees. He may charge costs of publicity for a group exhibition split among the artists showing. His "costs" may include his rent, light, and heat. Thus, a dealer of this variety knows ahead of time that he has his income guaranteed by *you,* and he does not need to bother about even trying to be an active dealer.

These are warnings for the professional artist. For there is indeed a reason for the existence of "non-professional" galleries. There are Sunday painters, amateurs, and retired businessmen who want very much to have a show, invite their friends, have a catalog to show the folks back home, and collect a few press comments from certain small publications which will write a "review" if the artist buys an advertisement. For these non-professional artists, probably the most direct and forthright dealers are the outright rental galleries who have a set fee for a certain amount of wall space.

Some of the others have fees that vary according to what they think the artist will put up with. Some of them go to many competitive shows, take notes on the artists who have no gallery affiliation, and write them, offering them shows and complimenting them on their great talent. Too often, professional artists are elated by this "recognition" and fall for the costly and "non-professional" show, which, in the long run, can be detrimental to the professional. Curators and press generally avoid these galleries, for their practices are known in the art field, and the "professional" gallery may be dubious about taking on an artist who has had his name affiliated with a "non-professional" dealer.

In case you want to show in Europe, don't be surprised if you find a quite different situation, for charging various fees is a much more commonly accepted practice.

It is pretty difficult to predict whether a dealer is going to be successful, or go out of business, or even go bankrupt. There have been cases in which artists were unable to retrieve their works from a bankrupt dealer because he placed everything from his gallery in a warehouse, where he already owed a large debt. Unless the artists paid his back bills, they could not obtain their works. In one recent case, a number of the artists kept an alert eye on their gallery's proceedings, realized the impending hazard of their dealer's situation, and took their works away.

Even outrageously obvious crooks have been able to pull the wool over unsuspecting artists' eyes for several years, before enough artists became sufficiently aware to put them out of business by not falling for the act. There was a dealer—fortunately now gone—who told artists that the way to start showing was in Europe; after this, they could walk into any gallery in New York and get a one-man show. How artists could have been so naive as to believe such a blatant misrepresentation is hard to understand, but quite a lot did. The dealer took three paintings from each artist, sent them abroad, arranged for some sort of minor press review (easily purchased abroad), and charged each artist $2,500. Many an artist borrowed widely from friends and relatives to pay this, believing that then he would be "made." The Art Information Center reported the dealer to the lawyers of the Art Dealers' Association and to the Better Business Bureau, but neither could do anything legally because, in each case, the artist had signed a statement that he agreed to precisely these terms. The Better Business Bureau could only send the dealer a notice that he was misrepresenting, and that, if asked, they would have to label him thus. But too many naive people do not think to check with the Art Information Center, nor with the Better Business Bureau, nor with the Art Dealers' Association.

The art gallery work force

The preponderance of dealers, even in the major art center of New York, started their galleries either alone or with only one part-time or full-time employee; and many still have the same sized staff even after five or more years. Although many others have increased their staffs over the years, they have usually added only one or two employees. Thus, this occupation is still perhaps more individual—in an old-fashioned "small business" concept—than most business operations today.

The question naturally arises: with so little assistance in the gallery, how much outside help must dealers employ? Actually, surprisingly little.

There are catalogs, brochures, announcements, press releases to be written. Most dealers particularly enjoy doing this kind of work themselves, and usually do.

There are shows to be installed and dismantled every three weeks during the art season. This they also do themselves, only occasionally hiring a carpenter in case of unusually heavy material or special construction needs.

There is layout and typography to think about for all printed matter. A tiny percentage of dealers hire a graphic design specialist, but by far the largest number work this out for themselves with their printers.

For traffic-transportation-shipping needs, they don't hire a traffic manager; they call up an art-trucking firm or, for imports, a customs broker.

For advertisements, the dealers work with agents; but this costs the dealer nothing, for agents get their commissions from the publications.

For accounting, dealers hire someone to come in quarterly. Obviously, government forms and checking the bookkeeping are aspects they do not relish, although they keep their own records in between the three-month visits.

Other outside help is likely to include a cleaning person; if the dealer is a woman, she is apt to prefer a cleaning man who can be pressed into service also for moving heavy objects and opening crates.

It becomes quite understandable, then, that dealers do not welcome shipments of work on speculation, for their facilities are so limited. And one of the biggest problems is lack of space, for suitable space is hard to find and very costly in every art area of every large city.

It is also natural that, since they do so much of the gallery work themselves, they do not welcome a constant flow of time-taking artists who walk into every gallery to show work without first taking the trouble to observe whether or not their work is at all suitable to the particular gallery's direction or style.

3

Shopping
for a
gallery

An artist is wise to take a little time away from his creative work to explore for himself what the galleries are showing and where he might fit.

What to read

One way is to read monthlies like *Arts* and *Art News* and *Artforum* and look at the reproductions with an eye to learning what kind of work is being shown in which galleries. *The Art Gallery*, which is primarily a monthly listing of gallery exhibitions in New York and various other U.S. cities, is also useful, particularly because it carries quite a number of reproductions. It is not complete, for it lists only those galleries which pay to be listed each month, and some dealers will not be bothered. So don't think that because a gallery is not found here that it has gone out of business.

Many newspapers have art columns. There are about 300 such newspapers listed in the *American Art Directory*, published every three years by R. R. Bowker Co., and available in good reference libraries. The papers are listed by states and cities, with the name of the art editor or critic in each case. Look up these art columns in your city, or in the city nearest to you, and become familiar with what is going on.

And, if possible, read the art pages of *The New York Times* on Saturday and Sunday. Although the *Times* covers mostly New York shows, except for out-of-town museum exhibitions, it may be helpful to you to become familiar with what is shown in New York, even if you do not plan to try to show there at first.

Go to see shows

In large cities, where most galleries are concentrated and where competition for clientele is sharpest, galleries are likely to specialize in some particular style or type of art expression. The best time to get a perspective on a gallery's direction is when it shows a few examples of work by each of its artists in a group show, so that you can get an over-all picture. Such shows are frequently held at the beginning and the end of the season, and prior to Christmas.

When you go to shows, make notes for yourself on what you saw where, including styles, media, sizes. If you keep systematic records of this nature, you will be in a much better position to sort out—from among all the galleries—where you might best try your luck. Some galleries show no sculpture; some show only smaller work—often because of the size of the gallery; some handle prints and drawings as well as painting and sculpture. These are things you need to know, in addition to the style or type of work a gallery handles.

Talk to people

If you know some other artists, some of them perhaps more experienced, pick their brains. Not infrequently, an artist who has a gallery affiliation has taken a friend to his dealer when he knew that there was an opening in the roster, and has thus placed him. But even if the result is not so direct, other artists may know more than you do about the reputations, practices, and availability of certain dealers. Add these impressions to your notes on galleries.

If you will study and analyze various galleries in this

way prior to asking them to look at your work, you will be in a much stronger position when you do select the galleries to try, for you will have a better awareness of where your work may find its proper surroundings and audience. One of the most discouraging aspects of a dealer's life is the fact that so many artists just barge in, with no regard for, or knowledge of, the gallery's direction. Indeed, some artists actually bring out slides of, say, landscapes to show a dealer when—if they would only look at the gallery display right around them—they could easily see the dealer exhibits kinetic sculpture.

An artist wrote to me from a New York suburb, complaining: "Most of the galleries seem to have turned to either Op, Hard-edge or some other crazy 'way-out' stuff, or 'pornographica.' Is there really no hope for artists like me, whose work is figurative but contemporary, yet not 'far out' or conservative?" It is a plaintive plea, but it is obvious that this artist neither reads much about shows in New York, nor goes to very many, despite his proximity.

I would guess that a similar lack of effort to inform himself afflicted the artist who wrote from Massachusetts: "Few months ago I spent a couple of days in New York 'trying to sell some paintings' to galleries who didn't know me from Adam. Needless to say I wore out a good pair of shoes for nothing. Someone gave me your address just before leaving but somehow you were out. Believe it or not, I didn't have enough money to stay one more day."

Shop locally first

If you live away from New York and have never had a show, you might be better off trying to get shown first in your nearest city, rather than trying to start off in the art center of the world, with no experience or background. Although some New York dealers are blase about the value of out-of-town sales and exhibitions, they nevertheless use such information as sales talks to potential customers. So before you make that expensive trip to New York, explore local possibilities; keep records of sales you have made and copies of press reviews you have received on local shows, of brochures and announcements, of collectors who have purchased your work. Some experience, no matter how modest it may seem to you, always looks better than none at all.

You never know when a New York dealer, shopping for new talent, may turn up in galleries elsewhere in the United States and abroad. If your local art dealer is alert, he will see to it that the scouting dealer has a chance to look at some of your work. Without such a local dealer, you would have little or no chance of being "discovered" by any New York gallery, for the traveling dealer generally goes to studios only after he has seen work of interest in a gallery. And how else is he going to know that you exist?

A great many artists in foreign countries write to me saying, "Please arrange a one-man show for me in New York." Frequently, they have obtained the name and address of the Art Information Center from the United States Cultural Attaché or from the United States Information Service officer in their country—individuals who don't know how to satisfy such requests any better than I do. In many cases, these artists have never even tried to exhibit at home; they actually seem to expect to start at the top, sight unseen. An artist in France writes: "I'm an American, but for the past several years have been living here in Provence. Although isolation is good for my work, it is bad in the sense that I have no outside contacts, therefore no way of selling my work, feeding my young family, and buying materials. How is an artist in my position without friends or contacts in New York ever to find a gallery to represent him? It's a great enough strain just to produce one's work. . . ."

Well, why doesn't he go to Paris, become familiar with some of the hundreds of art galleries there, and then try to show in one? As for the "great enough strain just to produce," I have never seen an artist who did not much prefer to stay in his studio, who did not hate to have to shop for a chance to show. It is just like anyone having to look for a job—that is the worst job in life. But it has to be done. However reluctant he may be to accept this fact, if he wants to exhibit, an artist must expect to take some time away from his studio work.

Start modestly

If you study and explore the gallery situation in the city where you would like to show, you will soon recognize the "top" galleries by their looks and size, by the kind of catalogs and announcements they issue, and by the size of the ads they take. If you have not yet attained a reputation, don't go to the top galleries and expect to make the grade— even if your work is in their direction. Being most in demand, such galleries are almost certain to have a full roster. When they do have an occasional opening, gallery directors are more likely to "steal" some artist from another, smaller gallery, where that artist has already made some reputation.

Explore the smaller galleries. Provided it functions on a correct professional basis, there is nothing degrading about showing in a small gallery, or in a gallery which is "off-beat" and not in the geographical area of the top galleries. Gallery-hopping is understandably a great outdoor sport for artists, for it is one way to get ahead and move from the smaller to the better-known gallery. Exposure is important: it is much better to show in a modest gallery than not to show at all. If you are successful there, you may be invited to move up.

A gallery which is newly forming may be worth looking into, for the dealer almost certainly does not yet have a full roster. It is impossible to predict how well he is going to make out or how long he will stay in business. But if you have a chance to talk with him and to gain impressions about his judgment and his taste in selecting his artists; and if you feel that you could have a good rapport with him, then you have little or nothing to lose by trying such a gallery. Many lasting relationships have developed between dealers and artists who started together on the ground floor. If the relationship doesn't work out and you must look elsewhere, at least you have built up some experience. Dealers, like artists, often start in a modest way. Then, if they are successful, they move into larger quarters in better art neighborhoods, taking their stable of artists with them.

Check the reliability of new dealers

Artists naturally like to check the reliability of new dealers, particularly when they are asked to send their work to a dealer who is about to open a gallery out of town. Many such dealers come to the Art Information Center to search for new talent. On the basis of the slides they are shown, they go to artists' studios and select work to display. Artists so chosen often call the Center to try to learn something about the reliability of the dealer. This is a very difficult question to answer, for there is no Dun & Bradstreet's for art dealer-to-be. I have sometimes suggested that the artist write to the curator of the museum in the dealer's city. The curator is likely to know something about the dealer if this individual has been active in the local art field. New dealers, in or outside of New York, would be wise to provide themselves with credentials, including letters or statements that would convince the Art Information Center and the artists of their reliability.

4

*Showing work
to dealers*

It scares dealers to see an artist entering his gallery with a big package or portfolio of original work. Dealers don't want you to set up your work in front of the show they have on their walls, for then customers will not know which is for sale.

Take slides

Dealers can look much more discreetly at slides of paintings or photographs of sculpture. If they are interested, they will suggest a time either for you to bring in originals or for them to visit your studio. If you have an unusual technique or combination of media which is only apparent in the original, then take along a relatively small original example, as well as the slide or photographic reproductions. Approximately fifteen to twenty slides of your best recent work is a sufficient number to take. If you arrive with boxes and boxes of slides, the dealer will be alarmed at the thought of having to take the time to look at them all. If you take only four or five slides, he will not get a sufficient feel of your style.

The 35 mm. color slide is most commonly used for this purpose. Artists who know little or nothing about photography nevertheless take their own, for it is very much less expensive than hiring a professional photographer—who often does not know much about photographing painting or sculpture. Artists who are strictly amateur photographers tell me that they get the best results by shooting their work outside, in daylight, when the sun is high. Apparently, the sun is the amateur photographer's best friend; artificial lighting is his Waterloo. I have seen many slides taken in the city showing a bit of roof or fire escape around the edges of the painting. It is a good idea to take two slightly different exposures of the same work when you have it set up; then you can select the better of the two for important use and still have a duplicate set on hand.

You are apt to have various needs for slides: a dealer may wish to keep slides for a day or two for consideration or to show to a partner; you may wish to send some to the Art Information Center for dealers to see when they go there seeking new talent; you may want to submit work to competitive shows or to curators of museums who ask to see slides first. You should have a complete additional set for yourself, for you never know when you may need them or if those you have sent out will return. As long as you have a full set on hand, you can always have duplicates mechanically made at the photography shop. Duplicates so made will not be quite as accurate in color and will usually cost a bit more than original duplicates, but they will nevertheless serve your needs.

Label slides and take a viewer

All slides and photographs should always be labeled with the dimensions of the work, the medium (if it is not immediately obvious from the reproduction), the title (if you wish to use a title), and your name. These notations should be made on the frame or margin in the direction in which the slides or photographs are to be viewed; thus, you indicate which way to put the slide in a viewer or which way to look at a photograph. Though most galleries and museums have viewers for 35 mm. slides, some don't. Therefore, it is wise to carry some kind of simple hand viewer. A projector which has to throw the image up on a wall may scare dealers as much as a huge parcel of originals, for it is equally indiscreet. There are numerous small viewers on the market; I prefer to use the type without batteries which simply utilizes daylight, for the colors in paintings are more true in daylight, and batteries have a tendency to peter out and make the light flicker. The daylight viewer, the most inexpensive kind, is often hard to find, for photography supply stores prefer to sell the ones that cost several times as much. But I find that with persistence, by placing an order, and then returning to remind the store about my order, I finally can get a daylight viewer. The stereoscopic viewer—which *does* work by battery—is particularly good for sculpture because it best conveys the three-dimensional aspects.

Take résumé

In many cases a dealer is more favorably inclined toward an artist if he knows that the artist has had some art experience and background. For the dealer understands that it will be easier to convince a vacillating, unsure purchaser if he can point out that your work has been exhibited here and there, has perhaps been selected by some well-known juror or institution, has perhaps won a prize or two.

For this reason, you should hand a brief résumé of your art background to the dealer along with the slides so that he immediately knows that you have had some experience in the field. Keep the résumé brief—a paragraph or a skeleton outline is enough. I have seen biographical material prepared by artists which went into long, flowery descriptions of philosophy and esthetics, making it difficult and time-taking to dig out any actual facts from the dissertation. Dealers do not have time for all this and they are not interested in your prose style; make it direct and easy for them.

Approaching gallery directors

A great many dealers dislike making advance appointments by telephone with artists they do not know. An important patron-customer might walk in just at that time, and then the dealer would be tied down by the appointment. To avoid this, they are apt to say, "We are booked up for the next two years," and that is the end of it; that door is closed to you. But if you just go—without an appointment—to a gallery you have selected as appropriate, you can observe whether the dealer is busy, either with a customer or with hanging a show and, if not, approach him. Do show consideration and tact; if the dealer is busy, go away and return another time. I sent an artist to a gallery that might well have proved suitable for his work; and when he got there, the place was being redecorated and in complete disorder. Nevertheless, this artist approached the dealer who said, "But we are painting the gallery; you can see the drop-cloths all over and the mess I'm in; come another time." In spite of this, the artist insisted, "I must see you now because I'm catching a train in forty-five minutes." The gallery director groaned and looked at slides, but it is unlikely that he would have taken on anyone at such a time. P.S. The artist did not get the job.

A certain number of dealers do prefer to make appointments with artists; if you go to their galleries without advance notice, they are more likely to look at their calendars and make a future appointment than if you use the impersonal telephone. If you have made a trip from some distance and can be in town only a few days, most dealers will considerately make the appointment within your time span.

Don't spurn a gallery assistant who may ask to see your slides before showing them to the director. A gallery assistant may be a "gal Friday" who pitches in on every aspect of the gallery's work; she is very seldom just a receptionist with no particular knowledge of the field. Assistants are by no means well paid; they work in galleries less for the money than because they have a vital interest in the field. Although they seldom have any final say, their interest and enthusiasm when they take your slides in to the boss may be distinctly to your advantage.

The best times to go to galleries are, naturally, when the directors are apt to be least busy. In New York, Saturday is the big gallery-going day for the public, so that is a bad day. On Monday, many galleries are closed. Tuesday through Friday is a better time unless it is apparent that a gallery is hanging a show and preparing for an opening.

Scheduled openings can usually be ascertained ahead of time from the listings of forthcoming shows in the art monthlies or *The Art Gallery*. Look up the gallery and don't go when an opening day is scheduled. Directors are not likely to be in their galleries before about 11:00 a.m. From then until about 2:30 p.m. is, perhaps, a better time than late in the afternoon, when customers are more likely to appear. This advice, however, is a rather vague generalization, for no one ever really knows what a customer is going to do or when he is going to do it.

Establish rapport with dealers

No two galleries are alike, and dealers cherish their individuality. So don't say to them, "I understand that all dealers" do this or that. Such generalizations will only get their backs up, and they will immediately point out how they differ, and how they function on their own quite independent terms and ideas. Don't quote to them the generalizations made in this book.

Unless you are really incapacitated, go yourself to see dealers; don't send a middleman with your slides. All too often an artist is delighted to get out of the ordeal when a wife, relative, or friend offers to go for him. But "mid-wives" are not generally welcomed; dealers want to know the artist directly, his thoughts and plans. Rapport between artist and dealer can be very important, but it cannot be established by a third person. Wives frequently say to me, "But my husband must stay in his studio and work; if I can find a gallery that shows interest, then he will go to see them." The trouble with this approach is that any potential interest is nipped in the bud.

Just as in any other field of operation, a letter of introduction or a reference from a mutual friend is, of course, useful in seeing a dealer. But with a dealer who is wrong for your type of work, even a letter is not sufficient reason to show your work to that dealer; when both you and he know your work is not suitable for his gallery, the situation can only be embarrassing.

Some dealers are more sympathetic than others

Many gallery directors are genuinely concerned about artists, realizing how many more good artists there are than the gallery space to exhibit them. "I have noticed," said one dealer to me, "how painful it is for an artist to have to go from one gallery to another. But we have virtually no space for a new artist unless one of ours leaves us or we decide we don't want to show him any more. I think this tight gallery situation should be explained to artists so they won't be too disappointed." To allay the disappointment, dealers often suggest other galleries they think are more suitable for the particular artist's work. Actually, it is unreasonable for an artist to expect such referrals; the dealer, busy with his own gallery, has no reason to be informed about the directions of his competitors. Hence, with the best intentions in the world, he may give you "bum steers."

I know one particularly sympathetic dealer who never refuses to look at artists' slides. In order to cope with this task, he asks artists to leave their slides overnight and then puts in many dedicated hours going over them after work. He estimates that about 600 artists come to him each season, many of whom are quite unsuited to his direction.

At the other end of the scale are some dealers who will not look at any artist's work. They have become too discouraged by the great waste of time involved. Most dealers fall between these two extremes and look at work some of the time—especially when there is a possibility that they might be able to exhibit a new artist.

If a dealer shows real interest in your work—and this is not hard to recognize—but regrets he has no room, then make a note to yourself to return to the gallery during the last half of May. (You might take slides of some new work as an excuse to remind the dealer of your existence.) Most contracts or agreements between dealers and their artists are for the season. If an artist is going to leave for another gallery the following fall, he must notify his dealer prior to summer vacation. Dealers usually make up their following season's schedule before they close for the summer. Even if an artist knows, say, in March that he is going to leave his gallery at the end of his contract, he is unlikely to create friction by saying so until near the close of the contract season. So a dealer is more likely to know about a gap towards the end of the art season than at any other time of the year.

5

Business terms
and
agreements

Always get a written receipt for any original work you leave on consignment with a dealer; asking for a receipt is not a reflection on his integrity, it is simply good business. This receipt is your *only* proof—otherwise it is your word against his.

Receipts and the law

In New York State, a law was passed in 1966 (amended in 1969) against absconding with any work of art, or the proceeds of sale, for which the artist holds a receipt. This law was promulgated by State Attorney General Louis J. Lefkowitz and by his expert in such matters, Joseph Rothman, with backing from Artists' Equity over the strenuous opposition of the Art Dealers' Association. Under this law a dealer can be prosecuted by the District Attorney for larceny if he wrongfully withholds an artist's work, or the proceeds of sale, left on consignment. Even if the dealer has left the state, he can be extradited for prosecution. Of course the enforcement of the criminal aspects of the law depends upon the functioning of the District Attorney, whose calendar is often loaded with cases he may consider more pressing than art. It would be helpful if district attorneys could be found with members on their staff who—like Joseph Rothman in the Attorney General's office—are serious artists in their spare time, so that they would give more sympathetic consideration to the artist's problems.

Nevertheless, this law takes a big step in the direction of protection for the artist, and New York is the first state to pass such legislation. Hopefully, art organizations, artists, dealers, and museums will press for legislative action elsewhere to implement protection for the artist throughout the nation. Meanwhile, if you have trouble in New York State with a dealer who has disappeared with your work, get in touch with your local district attorney or with the State Attorney General's office, 80 Centre Street, New York, N.Y. 10013. If you encounter difficulty with a dealer who is a member of the Art Dealers' Association, its legal division will give prompt attention to your complaint, for this association is most anxious to maintain a good public image.

For summaries of New York State laws dealing with the fine arts, see Appendix.

Insurance

When you consign work to a dealer, ask him what insurance value he can place on it. Some dealers carry no insurance on work while it remains in the gallery, leaving this responsibility entirely to the artist. But most galleries insure from 40% to 66 2/3% of value, and a very few to 100% of value. A great many artists carry art floater policies on their work so that, even though they are unlikely to have full-value coverage, they do have some additional protection on their own. The floater insures wherever the work is—in studio, gallery, friend's house, or truck.

If you know for how much the dealer will insure your work while it is in the gallery (often he will write this down on your receipt), then you can decide whether you wish to carry more or less supplementary insurance yourself.

Transportation

Shipping and cartage costs are almost always the artist's responsibility. Of course, in many cases the solution is simply a matter of borrowing a friend's stationwagon. But when a dealer in Montreal, for example, wants to show work by an artist in New York, he may well offer to pay transportation either both ways or one way. How many concessions he is willing to make depends on how eager he is to show the work. If a dealer is anxious to import large or heavy material from abroad, he may have to split shipping costs, which might otherwise be prohibitive for the artist.

Sculpture bases, frames, installation

Although many dealers supply all, or at least some, of the sculpture bases needed, virtually none supply or pay for frames. This practice is quite logical and understandable from a practical point of view, for a dealer who regularly shows sculpture will have bases on hand; whereas an artist who shows paintings has usually already framed them. Most installation costs are carried by the gallery. But if the nature of his work requires unusual or special equipment, the artist may be expected to bring it from his studio or to pay at least part of the cost of having it constructed.

Commissions

There are still galleries around the United States whose regular sales commission rate is 33⅓%, but they are becoming fewer and fewer. Most galleries, especially those in New York, charge 40%. Like everything else which has increased in price since World War II, dealers' costs have risen and so have their commissions. Be prepared, then, to pay 40% to your dealer on sales. If you find a reliable dealer who charges less, you are just lucky. Some dealers, who take care of part of the costs usually billed to the artist, take a still higher percentage. The few gallery directors who still charge a 33⅓% commission usually have to make up the difference in various additional costs to the artist. In most cases you can't win.

Work left on trial

Most dealers take work by living artists on consignment. This means that whether you are asked to leave work on a trial basis, for a group show, or for a one-man show, the dealer pays you nothing until the work is sold.

Remember that most established galleries are booked quite far ahead with one-man shows of work by their roster of artists. Probably the best they can offer you at first is the opportunity to leave a few things on trial. A dealer can properly handle only about two dozen affiliated artists because he is expected to give each of them a one-man show every two or three years, as well as hold two or three group shows of their work each season. This obligation fills the art season calendar, which runs, roughly, from late September to early June. If the dealer takes on too many artists, he cannot do right by them.

One long-established New York gallery found itself in a real predicament because its owner was too generous about taking on artists. When the owner died and his heirs took over, they found a roster of forty artists—meaning that each one could have a show only about every four years, which is just not enough exposure for an artist who has "arrived." The new owners frankly explained their dilemma to the artists, urging them to try to find another gallery. They offered to help their artists in every way possible and to continue to represent and back them until they could find an outlet that could give them better attention.

Even if you have previously held exhibitions elsewhere, a dealer generally wants to see how his particular clientele reacts to your work. If the dealer takes work on trial and sells some in two or three months, he will doubtless ask for more; if not, he will probably suggest that you take it back. He may not even hang it or show it publicly; he may have some particular customers in mind to invite to see the work in the gallery's back room. This way of proceeding can be of distinct value to the artist, for many of the best sales are made in the back room. Good customers can influence a dealer's decision about acceptance; sales often lead to a request from the dealer for more work to show out front.

Group shows

In addition to the annual group shows of work by their

regular artists, many dealers also hold group exhibitions of "guest" artists whose work interests them. These shows, frequently scheduled for off-peak seasons such as late May and June or early September, are also a kind of trial run to see how the new work will be received.

In a group show the work is definitely "out front" in the gallery. Moreover, the show is often publicized by the dealer; occasionally, there are some press notices about it. Success with such new work, in public and press response and in sales, can mean that you will be taken into the gallery's roster as soon as the next opening appears.

The artist who is asked to leave work either on trial or for a guest group show should not stop there. It is a good idea to continue to see all the galleries that you have analyzed as suitable for your work. Dealers who have your work on trial do not expect exclusivity. You are completely at liberty to try elsewhere at the same time, without building up any prejudice by so doing. You may get additional similar opportunities, thus achieving more exposure, and quite possibly more sales and recognition. Furthermore, you have a chance to see which gallery works best with your particular art form, and which has the better clientele for it.

One-man shows

Once you are asked to have a one-man show, the dealer doubtless wishes to consider you a regular member of his gallery's stable. Occasionally, there are guest one-man shows; but this is a rare event, for dealers are more apt to reserve this top recognition for artists who are definitely affiliated with them through some sort of contract or agreement.

Contracts

It doesn't matter whether a contract is printed in legal language, is made through an exchange of letters, or is verbally agreed on. In all cases, the contract is considered binding. One highly reliable dealer in New York wrote to me: "I have found that it is best to deal with artists on the basis of mutual understanding and trust. I do not believe in 'contracts' because a contract is only as good as the two people signing it. Since I would never sue an artist in court, I would not find a contract meaningful. However, for the artist's protection of his work, I insist upon giving the following agreement to each artist when he first joins the gallery." And there follows a pretty comprehensive set of arrangements.

Particularly for a newcomer, it is more satisfactory and protective to have something in writing. If your dealer has no contract or agreement form and you have merely discussed the terms of your agreement, go home and write a letter outlining what you feel to be your understanding of the agreement. Keep a carbon copy for yourself. If you have misunderstood or misrepresented any terms in the letter, the dealer will surely let you know the corrections. Keep these documents as your binding agreement.

Read every word of anything you sign. Some artists, elated at the thought of obtaining a one-man show or shy at the thought of seeming to doubt their "benefactor" dealer by scrutinizing the papers, have later found out some sorrowful factors to which they have bound themselves legally. Most good dealers will have more respect, not less, for the artist who takes time to go over a contract carefully, ask questions, and clarify points.

Artists' Equity Association, Inc., issues a form contract, a receipt form, and a bill of sale for the guidance of artists. You would do well to scrutinize these models. They are available from the Seattle headquarters, free to members. Keep in mind, however, that these forms are drawn up primarily from the point of view of the artist. Certain of their terms—such as complete coverage by the dealer of all costs of a one-man show, and full value insurance by the dealer—are rather more idealistic than realistic, for they are rarely achieved. For a typical contract form, see the Appendix to this book.

Terms of contracts

Terms of contracts or agreements should cover the following:

Length of period during which the dealer is to act as your sales representative: This is usually one year. Some dealers, however, prefer two-year agreements when the artist is relatively unknown. They feel that investments in publicity and groundwork laid during the first year do not pay off until the second.

Percentage commission to gallery on sales: This is generally 40% in the large art centers, but there are some areas where the old 33⅓% commission is still retained. If the commission asked by a dealer is less than the normal going rate, scrutinize other terms and costs to make sure that you are not paying too much out of pocket to make up the difference in the commission. A gallery which asks only 25%, for example, may not base its business on making many sales, an arrangement that is not to your benefit. A gallery asking a low commission can be even more suspect than a gallery which charges more than 40%. Some half-dozen of New York's big galleries which handle high-priced, well-known artists charge 50% to 55%. However, these galleries then take care of all costs, of widespread promotion, of show distribution, and of other activities for their artists.

Some contracts spell out the usually accepted agreement that the dealer receives no commissions on prizes or awards granted to the artist, but does receive commission on a purchase prize. Charitable sales are generally exempt from commission unless the artist has received his full price. Full price payment is unusual, for the soliciting charities customarily request that the artist split the sales price with them on a fifty-fifty basis or perhaps with 75% going to the artist. With the increased cachet of contemporary art in the world of society, these requests from charities have become so numerous in recent years that many dealers have clamped down on granting any of them—not only because they receive no commission on such sales, but also because they feel that their artists are being victimized. For the charitable organization ladies are all too prone to take the attitude: "We're not asking you for money, just for some of your work," with no apparent realization that an artist's work is his livelihood.

Sometimes an artist is taken in unwittingly by an "invitation" to enter a show, inclusion in which is presented as an honor. An artist friend of mine recently answered such an invitation from a well-known print club which said it had obtained exhibition space in an established New York print gallery. The invitation did not mention commissions. He sent a large engraving which he priced at $45. Soon he was notified that it had been sold. Later, he received a check for only $15, along with a statement that the gallery had taken one-third and the print club had taken another one-third. He said he certainly would never have sent the print had he known he was inadvertently making a "charitable" contribution to the print club.

The case of contributions of work to an art sale for a politician's campaign fund is entirely different. Dealers are not apt to intervene in an artist's political views or activities. And there are no proceeds at all to artist or dealer if an artist donates work for this purpose. For it is against federal law for anyone other than the campaigner to receive payment from any political campaign activity. The donation must be complete and total. I found this out unexpectedly when I ran an art sale for Adlai Stevenson in 1956. I was telephoning artists and naively suggesting a split on sales revenue between Stevenson and the artist, when an old-line Democratic politician came along and said, "You can't do that," and produced the law. I then called back all the artists, suggesting that under these circumstances they should just send a print, drawing, or small watercolor. Most of them contributed major works anyway—some as many as a dozen. And the cigar-smoking old-timers started to look around at "all this crazy modern stuff" when they heard the cash register ringing.

Extent of exclusivity: By geography, exclusivity varies according to the gallery's outside contacts. Often the exclusivity required is just for the city and its environs; you are free to show and sell anywhere else without paying your dealer a commission. Often, however, exclusivity covers the whole of the United States. Sometimes it is worldwide—particularly if the gallery has branches abroad or exchange arrangements with foreign galleries. Geographical exclusivity does not mean that an artist cannot show elsewhere. Out-of-town shows are often arranged either by the dealer or the artist. In these cases, your dealer must agree to the exhibition, and the out-of-town dealer must agree to give credit in the catalog to your dealer and to split the sales commission with him, usually on a 20%-20% basis, which means no extra charge to you. Occasionally, when commissions are to be split, the agreement is made that the artist will receive only 55%, the two galleries splitting the other 45%. Your dealer invariably expects you to pay him his full regular commission on sales you make from your studio, or on any other sales without the assistance of the gallery. You may give work to your friends, but you may not sell to them less the dealer's commission. Perhaps you wonder why. It is apparent that sales are definitely related to reputation, and your dealer, by showing your work and having your name promoted in connection with his gallery, has surely enhanced your chances for sales. Moreover, dealers have found out by sad experience that both collectors buying and artists selling are all too prone to bypass the dealer's commission, no matter how much work and effort he has expended.

Exclusivity terms may also specify media. That is, many galleries make exceptions in their totality of representation for work such as prints or other multiple productions. If their own chief interest lies in your major work, they do not want to take up time and space with many less expensive items. In such cases, they are quite willing to state that you may also be represented by a print or multiple gallery. Occasionally, galleries also waive their rights to small works; for some years there has been a gallery in New York for small paintings and sculptures only, every member of which must also have another, "regular" gallery in order to belong. This, of course, means that the regular gallery has given permission in each case.

Time of one-man show: The length of your show should be stipulated in your contract or agreement. Normally, a one-man show should run for about three weeks. Dealers have learned by experience that it takes about this long for the show to pay off after it has caught on. Sometimes dealers suggest 10-day shows, usually because they want to make at least part of their income from a fast turnover of fees from artists, part of which may go into their pockets instead of into legitimate costs for the artist.

Frequently the date, or at least the month, of the show is also stipulated. The usual times for scheduling one-man shows are October and November, and from January to mid-May. In December, most dealers have group shows of work by their affiliated artists, exhibiting small pieces, watercolors, prints, drawings—items likely to appeal as Christmas gifts. Now and then some expensive artists have refused to have their shows in January or February on the theory that too many well-heeled collectors are off in Florida at that time. But very few people feel that this is a serious consideration, particularly in view of the fact that nowadays winter vacations are taken just about any time during the winter season.

Many agreements also mention that, in addition to the one-man show, your work will always be represented in each gallery group show, and that a few works will be kept on hand, at all times, in gallery bins.

Prices and payments: Frequently, contracts state that after sales prices have been mutually agreed upon, nothing will be sold at a lower price without the artist's consent. Frequently also, it is stipulated that the money received by the dealer from sales is held in trust, and that payment will be made in a reasonable time—perhaps fifteen days after final payment, perhaps regularly once a month.

Commercial use of art and reproduction rights: Commercial uses of works of fine art are becoming more and more frequent. Artists and dealers, therefore, are increasingly aware of the need for protection. It is now fairly common for dealers to stipulate in their agreements with artists that they will at no time sell an artist's work with reproduction rights for commercial use unless such rights are additionally purchased, and then only with the artist's permission. Thus, if an artist does not wish to see his painting decorating an insurance company's promotion calendar, he can refuse to allow its reproduction even though the insurance company has purchased the painting. If he does not object to this arrangement, he will receive royalties or some other additional reimbursement. Many dealers require a commercial purchaser to sign an acknowledgment that the sale is made only on the understanding that all reproduction rights still belong to the artist. If the dealer has arranged the commercial sale, and if the artist gives his consent to reproduction, the dealer will expect 10% to 20% commission on the additional funds. There are cases, such as for educational uses, when charges for reproduction rights are waived by the artist and his dealer, who are glad to help some professor illustrate his textbook. But this decision is entirely up to the artist under the usual contract clause covering this contingency.

Although in recent years these protections have become fairly widespread and have been fostered and promoted urgently by such organizations as Artists' Equity, they are still not as accepted as artists might wish. In New York State, the Act of September 1, 1966, states: "Whenever a work of fine art is sold or otherwise transferred . . . the right of reproduction is reserved to the grantor . . . unless expressly transferred in writing signed by the owner of the rights. . . ." This kind of legislation also needs to be more widespread.

Expenses: In addition to suitable framing, some transportation costs, and insurance expected of all exhibiting artists, the contract usually states that the artist must pay all publicity expenses—but for a one-man show *only*. These expenses will probably be the largest of all (they are likely to average about $600 in New York). But you are not apt to achieve a one-man show until you have already sold work left on trial or have exhibited in a group show (where you should not pay for publicity). Consequently, you probably won't have to face the publicity costs of the one-man show until after you have collected some funds to defray them.

Publicity costs usually include advertisements, a brochure with some reproductions, mailing charges, photographs for the press, and in some cases, an invitation and preview.

Charges should not include rent, light, heat, or secretary's salary. You should be able to see the actual bills for these out-of-pocket expenditures and to know just where your money went.

In many cases, the dealer will consult the artist's wishes regarding publicity and will accordingly place larger or smaller ads, prepare an elegant or simple brochure, and cut down on or eliminate the preview to accomodate the artist's pocketbook and desires. But in many other instances, dealers have contracts with publications for ads and these must be fulfilled; they have a regular size and format for brochures to be published in similar form as a kind of "signature" of the gallery; they have a standard form of preview. In such cases, you are not in a position to dictate or argue; you have to take it or leave it, for the dealer is privileged to run his gallery as he sees fit. If you cannot afford the particular dealer's outlay on publicity, then you must try to get another dealer with a less "elegant" approach. The contract generally demands these payments in advance, so you cannot wait for sales from your forthcoming show to take care of them.

There is a very wide range in outlay for publicity among New York galleries. The costs per show (which I have obtained from a couple of dozen selected reputable galleries, large and small, old and new) indicate: for advertisements, a range from $75 to $3,000; for brochure, from $60 to $1,800; for mailings, from $40 to $500; for invitation and preview, from zero (where they have none) to $700 (up to $200 for invitations and up to $500 for preview).

What the artist must pay for publicity also varies according to his reputation and his sales record. The better known and the more financially successful you become for yourself and your dealer, the more likely he is to absorb at least some of the costs.

Contracts frequently state that the dealer agrees to pay for packing and shipping work to clients, and mentions the percentage of total value he is willing to insure for, against loss or damage in the gallery only.

Cancellation of agreement: Most contracts are binding to the end of the stipulated period. At that time they may or may not be renewed by a further agreement. Some dealers, however, state that the contract may be cancelled by either party with a stipulated amount of notice, provided that printing for a show has not already been done and advertisements have not already been placed.

Preliminary arrangements for a one-man show

Once the contract is signed, your dealer will probably come to your studio and select the work he wants to include in your show. Usually, he will discuss the selection and be guided by your judgment, as well as his own. I have known of cases, though, like that of an artist noted for his sculpture, who also wanted to exhibit his paintings. The dealer refused, feeling that the artist was inferior in his more recently developed medium and believing that showing this work would only be damaging to both their reputations. Some years later, in another gallery, the artist had his way; the general critical evaluation indicated that the first dealer had been acute in his prediction.

You may have to send most of your exhibition items to the gallery a month or six weeks before its opening so that critics of the art monthlies can preview them. Critics must see work this far in advance if their reviews are to appear at the time of your show. Most reviewers do not have time to go to studios. If the gallery is cramped for storage space, you may have to take the work back to your studio again until time for its installation. Although your dealer will have a mailing list not only of press, but of customers, he will undoubtedly request your own mailing list of friends and collectors or will ask you how many additional brochures you want printed to send to your mailing list. In many cases, artists mail out their own lists, often adding notes of a personal nature to the brochure or announcement mailed.

Your dealer may wish to expand somewhat your brief résumé for biographical information to appear in the catalog and press release, and to use any good quotations available from your reviews. He will expect you to provide quality 8" x 10" glossy photographs of a half dozen works to be shown, perhaps with three or four copies of each. For this purpose it is probably advisable to use a professional photographer. The photographs will be mailed to a few selected publications in hopes that they will be reproduced; others will be kept at the gallery for critics who may come to your show.

Dealers often welcome the assistance of the artist in installing a show. Time is very short: in a typical situation, the previous show closes on Saturday at 5:30 or 6 p.m.; your show opens on Tuesday afternoon. All dismantling and disposal of the previous show, refurbishing of gallery walls (nail-holes, paint scratches), as well as complete installation and labeling of your show must be done on Sunday and Monday. Occasionally, however, a dealer has his own special way of working or a special display technique, preferring to install the show by himself, with assistance from just his own staff.

For your preview there may be a party at which drinks are served, but just as often there is no party. While Tuesday is the most common opening day in New York, this day is by no means mandatory. Although many galleries are normally closed on Mondays, some have their previews that evening. The time is usually from 5 p.m. to 7 or 7:30 p.m. Because Saturdays are the biggest gallery-going days for public attendance, some dealers who do not wish to hold parties or stay open into the evening simply announce that their new shows will have their openings on Saturdays, throughout the day.

When parties are held, the preview costs may include overtime for an elevator operator and perhaps the hiring of a bartender, though more often the latter capacity is filled by a gallery assistant or a friend. Hard liquor and snacks are sometimes served; sometimes just a glass of sherry or wine. The party has become something of a problem because of the "floater" and "hanger-on" element which drifts from one gallery party to another just for free drinks. There is actually a firm in New York which, for a "subscription" fee, will tell you by phone where free drinks are being served tonight. Frequently, when leaving a gallery opening, you will hear someone announce, in an elevator full of gallery-goers, "They are serving hard liquor at such-and-such gallery." Naturally, both dealer and artist would prefer to be delivered from the floater elements and the costs incurred by them, as well as the beatnik atmosphere often imported by them. Some galleries wishing to hold parties issue invitations which must be shown at the door; others avoid the problem by serving nothing. In the latter case, it is not uncommon for the dealer or the artist to invite friends to cocktails or a buffet supper, at home or in a restaurant, thus entertaining only those whom they wish to honor.

Outright purchases

Very few "art dealers" buy work outright from living artists. Some occasionally buy work by artists in their own roster for their personal collections. A few make purchases from their artists in cases of need. A few buy on a monthly payment basis as a kind of advance to an artist. In such a case—which is rare—if the work is later sold, the dealer takes half the sales price and deducts from the artist's 50% whatever payments have already been made to him.

In the low-priced market, there are "picture" dealers who buy outright for quick, inexpensive turnover. Perhaps the largest and most widespread is Arts International, Ltd., with headquarters at 59 Walton Street, Chicago, galleries in numerous cities of the United States, and offices in five European capitals. Their sales prices range from $5 to $75, including their commission, so the artist is lucky if he gets half this amount. For prolific producers this arrangement can still mean income, as it doubtless also does to foreign artists to whom dollars are worth more than in the United States. There are also numerous frame shops which buy paintings, drawings, and prints to display and sell with their frames, often with a sign: "This picture with any frame in the window—$75." Naturally, such purchasers will try to obtain the artist's work at the lowest possible price.

Critics and reviews

Critics are people whom everyone shakes a fist at, except on the rare occasion of a good review. Not that critics always, or even most of the time, write bad reviews; it is just that they don't write any at all about so many shows. There are too many shows and too few critics. In New York there may be 85 or 90 openings in one week during peak season. All the artists and all the dealers want their shows reviewed by *The New York Times*. The *Times* has three reviewers who must cover museum exhibitions—frequently outside as well as inside New York—and also do what they can about the many gallery shows.

How to get on their priority list is a chronic dilemma. Many different approaches are tried: irate letters to the editor; needling telephone calls to the art department; a plethora of photographs and other material bombarding them in the mails; pleading and wheedling, excoriating and threatening. Critics nevertheless go their way, probably with no priority lists at all and with no regard for these numerous appeals. Often it is apparent that to some extent they go their way geographically, for reviews of shows will appear on galleries which are geographically close: one may assume that critics' feet get tired too. No matter how critics select what they cover, there are always many artists and dealers who are certain that their shows were far more worthwhile and deserving than those reviewed. Old-timers consequently tend to relax, shrug their shoulders, expect nothing. If a review does happen to appear, it is a great and unexpected event.

Some monthly art magazines are much more inclusive. *Art News* covers every one-man show, but usually not group shows. They may cut the review to just a few lines, but they give it some sort of space. *Arts* reviews more than four-fifths of New York shows. *Artforum*, which started on the West Coast but later moved its headquarters to New York, now reviews some thirty major New York shows each month, selected on the basis of what the editors consider most important. Weeklies such as *New York, The New Yorker, Cue, Time, Life, Newsweek,* and *Look* generally select a few highlights in the art area. The more widespread the distribution of the publication, the more it attempts to reach outside New York for its stories. And in some cases the publications are more interested in the "story" than they are in the merit of the art.

Many of these publications carry listings of openings as an editorial service, not paid for as an ad. Usually, it is not hard to get a show listed if the information is sent before the deadline; and these listings, even if they make no critical comment, do help to guide people to your show.

A number of little publications in New York will carry reviews if the shows are advertised in their papers. Although some people turn up their noses at this kind of coverage, it can be useful. I know a Midwest artist-teacher who was told he could not get a promotion or increase in salary unless he had a New York one-man show during the season—a form of "publish or perish" edict transferred to the art field. He was able to get a show in a small gallery and a couple of reviews in small weekly papers—sufficient evidence for the Midwest authorities to give him his promotion. Fortunately for the artist, they doubtless did not even know that such reviews were available to anyone as long as advertisements were placed.

Probably the best of these little New York papers, with the most knowledgeable art critics, are *Park East, Aufbau* (in German), *France-Amérique* (in French) and, for shows in Greenwich Village and the East Village, *Village Voice* (*Village Voice* does not assure a review for an ad).

In cities other than New York, it is usually a bit easier to get some kind of review or news story in the local press. Facing less competition and concentrated art activity, your dealer has a better chance to get coverage from the publication's local critic.

You should put copies of whatever write-ups you get, along with other printed material such as brochures, announcements, and press releases about your work, into a portfolio. You never know when you may want to approach another dealer; although some dealers want only to look at work, others do want to see such records when considering the possibility of handling your work. Some dealers like to keep portfolios of this nature in the gallery to show to prospective customers.

Commissions for murals, portraits, architectural sculpture, monuments

Alert dealers always keep an ear to the ground for possible commissions for their artists, and many have mailing and telephone lists of architects and interior designers to use when appropriate. But don't count on it. If you know any architects likely to commission sculpture, murals, or monuments in a vein that harmonizes with your work, check with your dealer to be sure he is making contact with them. Don't go to them directly unless you first arrange to do so with your dealer, for you then might duplicate and interfere with his efforts, and he would be justifiably angry. Once you have a dealer representing you, it is always you who must check with him before making any move aimed at contacts for sales. For this is his province, so he is expected to go about his business without checking with you.

Periodically two or three architects from an important firm "go shopping" in galleries for art to enhance a new building project. Such a visit usually puts the dealers into a tizzy of delight, with great hope for "something big" to result. It is amazing how small the art world in big New York can be. Word of these visits usually spreads like wildfire, and the architects are bombarded with calls from dealers not visited: "Please come to see my artists."

A number of galleries have developed in New York especially to serve the interior design and decorator field. For the most part, they are located in that area of the city—roughly from 57th to 65th Streets between Lexington and First Avenues—where many entire office buildings are devoted to interiors, from period to modern. Some of these dealers have their own rosters of artists, give one-man shows, and operate as regular galleries. Others show work by artists with different gallery affiliations, split commissions on sales, never give one-man shows, and concentrate on placing work in "the trade." Many also show unaffiliated artists, but these galleries ask no exclusivity. Frequently these specialty dealers sell in quantity—for example, to a firm buying a painting for each office on three entire floors of the Pan Am Building. They also obtain mural commissions for new hospital wings and new apartment buildings through working with the interior design consultants for the buildings.

Apparently not all such consultants always consult. In one instance, a large abstract mural was commissioned for the entire length of the lobby in a new apartment building. Two weeks after installation, the landlord appeared for the first time, gave forth the edict that it was horrible, and ordered it completely covered with canvas. The tenants then complained bitterly: they did not like canvas, they did like the colorful abstract mural. The tenants won. The canvas cover came down. The artist had already been paid; even so, he naturally was much happier to have his work seen and to receive "popular" backing for it.

Many of the firms selling furniture and interior accessories also welcome the opportunity to display some paintings and sculpture suitable to their line. They may borrow from art galleries and refer purchasers to them, asking no commission. They may show and sell work by unaffiliated artists if the work seems to have a rapport with their display rooms. Price labels are attached so their customers know the art is for sale; and when they sell, they take only a small commission, such as 10%, for handling costs. If these displays lead to commissions, the artist usually takes over on his own, with a nice "thank you" to the furnishings firm. Sometimes interior decorators make purchases for their clients directly from an artist who has no gallery agreement; payment in some instances may be very good.

In cases of some architectural sculpture and murals, it is often the architects themselves who commission. Some years ago, they apparently were at a loss to know how to go about this. One well-known head of a large architectural firm called me about a huge sculpture he wanted to place outside a high-rise office building; it must be big enough not to look dwarfed by the building. Where could he go to see work from which to select? Since this obviously called for a sculpture several stories high, I pointed out to him that he could scarcely expect to find already completed work in sculptors' studios, that he would have to commission such a piece. He could start with several sculptors whose work seemed suitable and ask for a maquette from each. Of course, he must pay for all the maquettes; but then he could choose the one which looked best beside the scale model of the building and commission that one for execution, with no further obligation to the other artists who submitted maquettes.

Today architects are much more aware of these procedures, for it has become *de rigueur* for buildings of any importance to contain works of fine art. Moreover, museum curators in recent years have often aided architects in these matters, in exchange for a tax-deductible contribution to the museum. Also, the American Federation of Arts now offers a regular consultant service of this nature to architects and business firms of all kinds. These activities have helped to spread commissions among many artists; formerly there was a great tendency to employ the same ones over and over. A firm desiring a sculpture on its building was loathe to stick its corporate neck out in a field unknown to it, and hence would hire the same sculptor already used by other firms because he seemed "safe."

The Business Committee for the Arts, with former Secretary of the United States Treasury, C. Douglas Dillon, as Chairman, was established in 1967 to act as a catalytic agent between business firms and the arts. A good deal of its attention focuses on the performing arts. However, Dillon manifests considerable interest in projects that give artists insight into new technological media by having them work with corporations which have the related facilities. In cooperation with the Los Angeles County Museum, twenty local firms each invited an artist to participate in a three months' residency, with just such aims in mind. The work which will result is to be exhibited in the Los Angeles Museum in 1970.

Dillon proposes other collaboration between art and business, specifically that artists be appointed by leading companies "to a new post in the department of public affairs, with a broad assignment to investigate possible arts projects and relate them to other aspects of a firm's public service program . . . this could have an incalculable effect on our country's cultural endeavor as a whole." (No. 5, *Cultural Affairs,* quarterly, published by Associated Councils of the Arts, New York, N.Y. 1969, p. 11.)

Further developments relating business and the arts are sure to be a part of the future. If these potential opportunities interest you, follow the local press to learn what is happening in your geographic area. These developments will undoubtedly be publicized and reported. The firms involved will see to that: they have energetic publicity offices, and they are good advertisers.

There are various organizations which help artists to obtain commissions. One is the National Sculpture Society, 250 East 51 Street, New York, N.Y. 10022, which holds competitions and exhibitions (especially of architectural sculpture), accepting work by non-members for some of its shows. Another is the National Society of Mural Painters, 41 East 65 Street, New York, N.Y. 10021, which holds biennial exhibitions and gives prizes to young artists for work related to architecture. The Architectural League of New York puts on frequent shows in the building of the American Federation of Arts, also at 41 East 65 Street, displaying work related to architecture, city planning, and subway station design. Portraits, Inc., 136 East 57 Street, New York, N.Y. 10022, is a gallery with a roster of artists specializing in portrait painting; in addition, the gallery also acts as agent for mural commissions.

In spite of the enormous invasion of photography into the field, portraits in the various media are still commissioned quite frequently. Although many galleries show occasional portraits along with other kinds of work by their artists, only Portraits, Inc. specializes in this field in New York. It is probably a safe guess that portrait painters and sculptors obtain more commissions on their own than they achieve through dealers. Portraiture is a field which is perhaps more self-generating than any other; because of the personal nature of the portrait, the satisfied subject is apt to become your best salesman, and one commission tends to lead to another.

The dealer's percentage

The percentage charged by dealers on outside commissions varies considerably, usually in proportion to how much the dealer contributed to obtaining the commission for the artist. If he was entirely responsible for it, he will probably expect the same 40% as on other sales. If he advances cash to the artist to enable him to work on the commission, he may expect 50%, as in other situations where the artist receives an advance. In some cases, where there are exceptional costs to the artist for materials or assistants, the dealer may take less or he may base his percentage on the net amount of the commission after expenses. If the artist obtained the commission entirely on his own, his dealer may expect only 10% or 15%, though in some cases galleries require 33⅓% on all commissions, regardless of their role.

Special portfolio

If you want to work on commissioned projects, you will be wise to prepare and keep a special portfolio up to date. This portfolio should contain reproductions of commissioned work already executed (if any), as well as of proposals, sketches, maquettes, and other pertinent material, including portraits if you are a portrait painter. If you cull this specialized work from your total output, you or your dealer can use the portfolio as a presentation.

Reproduction rights

Many artists now insist on labeling the back of every painting, "All reproduction rights reserved," and require this statement on every invoice. When commercial firms purchase paintings along with reproduction rights (providing the artist consents), they frequently do so on the basis of an outright sum which is perhaps double or triple the price of the original work. This procedure avoids the complicated book-keeping required by a royalty-on-sales agreement; assures the artist of immediate payment of a specific amount; and removes any doubts he might have about the accuracy of the bookkeeping.

Unlike the field of book publishing, there is no rule of thumb, no standard arrangement, as to the amount paid for reproduction rights, whether a flat sum or a royalty. So much depends on the size and sales price of the reproduction, as well as on the distribution and promotion of the commercial firm, that each case is an individual matter.

The New York Graphic Society Ltd., a subsidiary of Time Inc. and the largest of the reproduction houses, never purchases outright the paintings it wishes to reproduce. Instead, it negotiates for reproduction rights to issue one edition of 1,500 to 2,500. For any additional reprinting, further permission must be obtained from the original source. 80% of the Graphic Society's arrangements are made by paying a fixed fee. Though payment varies according to considerations such as saleability, it is not predicated on the name and fame of the artist. In the remaining cases where the company pays a royalty, this sum is figured at 5% of the average wholesale price of the reproduction. This amount is calculated to be 50% plus 33⅓% off the established retail price, for the distributor must get his one-third, and the retail price is normally twice the wholesale price. Therefore, if a print sells for $12.00, the artist's royalty on each sale will be 5% of $4.00, or 20 cents.

All reproductions are copyrighted. If the painting reproduced belongs to a museum or private collector, the Graphic Society pays nothing to the owner other than a token number of *gratis* copies of the reproduction. If a work belongs to a museum whose name will appear on the reproduction, the museum's permission, as well as the artist's, must be obtained. If a reproduction is to be used in a firm's promotion piece that is to be given away, both the museum and the artist should have the right to see its preliminary layout and copy so that they may determine whether it is sufficiently dignified. Generally, then, the piece must be geared for a prestige type of promotion, not for product advertising. Both the artist's and the museum's names should appear in conjunction with the reproduction, and on the same page, not in a credit box somewhere else in the publication. Because such uses are usually predicated on the prestige value of the museum's name, and because museums are proverbially in need of funds, the museum frequently requires the firm to pay to it a sum equal to that paid to the artist for these rights.

Reproductions in periodicals

Of course no charge is made in the event that reproductions are to be used in conjunction with a critical review, or for other publicity purposes which are eminently to the advantage of the artist. Indeed, your dealer should make every effort to have your work reproduced free of charge as often as possible in art columns, catalogs, journals, and books. Without question, such reproduction actually raises the value of the work of art and the status of the artist.

However, some periodicals tend to exploit the concept of "publicity" for the artist, when actually they wish to use reproductions of works of art primarily as free illustrations for texts not related to the artist. They don't want to pay or commission an illustrator for the job; in order to avoid paying an artist for reproducing his work, they will argue that the name credit they give him is sufficient reward because of its publicity value—a very dubious premise. The more reliable periodicals, however—such as *The New York Times* Sunday Book Review Section—have long since established the precedent of paying an artist at least a small fee for using his work to illustrate their articles. Here again, it should be ascertained that the reproduction will be used in a dignified context and that credit to the artist will appear on the same page as the reproduction. Surely if more artists and their dealers, as well as more museums owning work by living artists, continue to demand fair payment and credit, the reproduction field will cease to be the racket it used to be and will supplement the incomes of some artists.

6

Pricing
and
selling

Dealers will often ask you what price you want to place on your works. If you have sold only from your studio or in smaller metropolises, you may not know just how to do this. Obviously, the dealer is interested in asking as high a price as possible, for then his commission will bring him more revenue. It is also apparent that a dealer knows his own customers' pocketbooks better than anyone else. Since the interests of the dealer are the same as yours—to get as good a price as possible—your best bet may be to ask and take his advice on the matter. The dealer knows that he cannot overprice work by unknown artists; he realizes he can push up prices after successes; and he understands the range of his customers' buying habits. Some dealers have more wealthy clients than others; if pricing seems too low to you, it would be better to go to other dealers than to argue.

Pricing

Most of the artists I see are fairly modest, when they start out, as to what they think their work is worth on the market. Occasionally I run into someone who has grandiose ideas. One man told me that he had never exhibited and never sold, but that he would take nothing less than $3,000 for one of his paintings. Would I please find him such a gallery? My reaction was that he would do better to hang his paintings on his own walls, instead, and to enjoy his expensive collection. Another artist, an unknown Florida painter, wrote: "I have about 200 primitive oil paintings, some in hand-made frames. Could you please give me the address of a gallery that might be interested in buying them? Have sold some of my paintings [for] $8500. . . ." One could only wonder, if true, why he would bother to try for a New York gallery.

On the other side of the fence are the novices in art buying who often expect a great deal for very little. A housewife called me from Queens to say she saw a beautiful painting, all framed, of a head of a gypsy. It was selling for $75. "Do you think if I buy it, it will be worth ten times as much in two or three years?" She had been reading about top auction prices for Impressionist works and jumped to the conclusion that fabulous increases in value applied to all painting. Nor is this too surprising in view of the fact that much commercial promotion of art in recent years has used just such rare examples of increases "far greater than any stock or bond on Wall Street" as a hard-sell approach: "You, too, may make a killing!" Another inquiry came to me from some graduating students at a Massachusetts college: "We are considering a class gift for the school and would like any available informaton on statues. We would like something that could be placed as a centerpiece on the main quadrangle as a possible portrayal of the contemporary period. Our funds are limited to a $200 to $400 price range." One hopes that after their commencement, they commenced to learn a few practical facts—even if only about costs of materials, not to mention the livelihood of artists.

Although many agreements and contracts allow no changes in prices mutually set by artist and dealer, this rule does not always apply. Especially when work is left on trial, dealer and artist may come to an understanding that prices will roughly fall within a certain range, and that the dealer will get the most he can by haggling within that margin.

Discounts

Museums and collectors: Artists and dealers alike must anticipate demands from certain quarters for discounts. All museums expect to buy at a discount, not only because they are non-profit educational institutions, but also because they know a museum acquisition enhances both the reputation and the market of an artist. In the past couple of decades, the generally accepted museum discount in New York has been reduced from 15% to 10%. Occasionally, however, galleries will give a little more when trying to get a new artist "put on the map."

Another category of discount buyer is the large collector who frequently buys in quantity. Just about every artist and dealer wants to be represented in certain well-known collections. A noted example is the collection of Joseph Hirschhorn, who for many years has extensively bought work by relatively unknown contemporary artists, often purchasing a score or more by the same artist. Many artists have been launched by these purchases and many have subsequently become well known. The collection—and a museum to house it—has now been given to the nation in Washington, D.C., with Alan Lerner, Mr. Hirschhorn's long-time curator, as first Director. For an artists' work to be a part of the Hirschhorn Collection has been for many years as advantageous to his sales as to be represented in a museum. Consequently, the same 10% discount is customarily applied.

Many big collectors agree to bequeath their art to a particular museum. The liberal tax allowances—even during the collector's lifetime—by the Internal Revenue Service have encouraged such procedures and are responsible for much privately owned work passing into the public domain. In this practice the United States compares very favorably with many other countries where, even when an art treasure is willed to a museum, the heirs must still pay inheritance tax on it. In many cases, therefore, the allowance of a discount to collectors is tantamount to a museum discount, for the works are pledged to wind up in museums.

Other discounts: Most dealers also give a 10% discount to educational institutions other than museums, such as universities, colleges, libraries. Many give preferential prices on purchases by other galleries, and as a commission to architects and decorators buying for their clients. Not infrequently, an artist or student purchaser is allowed a discount; I know one dealer who will take off 10% for an eager purchaser if he is poor. Though I am puzzled about how the "means test" (or gauge of pocketbook) is applied, I do know that I have benefitted by this kindly attitude. Discounts may also be offered by a dealer when he is selling off inventory.

Sales from the studio

Lots of people prefer to purchase directly from an artist's studio, rather than from his gallery. Often this preference simply stems from a desire to see and talk with a real live artist, and to get in behind the scenes; it makes prestigious cocktail conversation about their purchase. Creative artists often fill many people with awe. Artists respond to this adulation in reactions that range from total rejection of such invasions and interruptions, to long-suffering toleration, to a pleased and friendly welcome.

Another big reason why purchasers prefer to visit an artist's studio rather than go to his gallery is to try to persuade the artist to sell without the dealer's commission, promising that they won't tell. This tactic, of course, violates all artist-dealer commitments. Nevertheless, a cagey buyer figures it will be easier to twist the arm of an unbusinesslike artist than to bicker with his professional dealer.

At the Art Information Center, I often receive calls asking for an artist's address. Unless the artist has no gallery affiliation, I give out only the name and address of his dealer. Compilations such as *Who's Who in American Art* and the *International Directory of Arts* do publish artists' addresses, but many purchasers either don't seem to know these sources or don't want to go to look them up in the library. And I never suggest these reference works. To mention the fact here is, I hope, "safe" because this book, directed to artists and dealers, is not likely to be read by collectors. The by-passing procedure by a collector is not only unfair to the dealer, but is also a burden, an embarrassment, and a nuisance to the artist.

Dealers themselves frequently make appointments with their artists for purchasers to visit studios, with the understanding, of course, that no price dickering will ensue. For practical reasons of space, the dealer may have only a few of the artist's works on hand; the purchaser may wish to see more before making a selection. This is the acceptable way in which sales are made from an artist's studio with integrity.

Installment buying

For many years galleries have sold on the installment plan, and virtually all galleries continue to do so. Losses from this arrangement have proved to be virtually nil.

I remember making a fairly comprehensive telephone check among New York dealers on this subject when I was Publicity Director of the Museum of Modern Art in New York. The Museum was then thinking of establishing its art lending library—a potential form of installment purchase, for the borrower can subtract rental fees from purchase price if he later decides to buy. Not one of the dealers I called was unwilling to sell "on time"; and not one had ever lost on such sales, although they sometimes had to wait as long as two years for final payment—even, occasionally, on a total of only $600 to $800.

Apparently, people who want to buy contemporary art are not swindlers. Possibly the individual and personal experience of buying work by a living artist is more exacting than dealing with a big impersonal corporation. Six psychologists would probably come up with six other theories. Whatever the reason, it is to be hoped that nothing— especially this report—will encourage swindlers to move in and change this happy situation.

Many dealers stipulate a time limit on long-term purchases, from six months to two years; but some simply state "open" or "extended." I once arranged to buy a $125 lithograph from a gallery which required no down payment whatsoever. But I did pay a first installment of $50 and asked the dealer to hold the print until I could accumulate the rest of the funds. He was actually angry. "I don't care if you don't pay anything now," he said, "but please you must take it home because I might forget and sell it again. And anyway I don't want it cluttering up my limited storage space."

Before making the arrangement, dealers selling on time are apt to consult with the artist to ascertain whether he will accept delayed payments; most artists do. In some cases, the dealer agrees to pay the artist in full at the time of the first installment and himself to wait to be reimbursed from the subsequent sums.

Unfortunately I must record one recent exception to the above rosy report; it is one which brings up a curious and rather surprising legal aspect. A dealer sold an artist's painting on credit, but was unable to collect either payment or the painting from the purchaser. Artists' Equity took the painter's case to the Attorney General's office, only to find that it was the artist who had to sustain the loss if the dealer could get neither the money nor the painting. Legally, the dealer, who did not get his commission, has already sustained his share of the loss. The artist could sue the dealer for negligence in checking his client's credit; but if he did, he would probably spend a lot more for legal costs than he originally lost in the price of his painting. One can only hope that this case is the exception which proves the rule.

Returns

Purchasers who want to return works of art for cash may not be successful in their efforts, for once the dealer has paid the artist, bookkeeping becomes complicated; and more likely than not the money has been spent. But dealers do make allowances for purchasers who go home with a painting or sculpture and immediately discover that it doesn't "live with" according to their expectations: art can look very different in different surroundings. Some dealers will return cash if the work is brought back within a month. More often, credit is extended or an exchange is arranged.

A purchaser will probably encounter no difficulty if he wants to exchange the unwanted piece for another, more expensive work by the same artist, and if he is willing to pay the difference. This practice is not infrequent, both for private collectors and for museums. The New York Museum of Modern Art, for example, buys many works by living artists on the understanding that they may later be exchanged for more recent works, often at additional cost; thus it can remain a museum of "modern" art. But never does the Museum turn in works by living artists if this means that these artists will no longer be represented in the Museum collection. Once an artist has achieved the right to say that his work is owned by the Museum, it would be manifestly unfair and harmful to his professional standing to deprive him later of that right.

7

Publicity

In New York it is widely agreed that the most valuable advertising medium is the Sunday *New York Times*. The Sunday edition has much broader distribution in the nation than does the daily, and dealers have found that its ads draw more attention and results than any other publication. The *Times* also has a Saturday page of art reviews and, Saturday being the biggest gallery-going day, New Yorkers frequently use this page as a guide for their visits. Hence, for local purposes, many dealers also advertise on Saturday. To encourage this practice, the *Times* offers a "tie-in" discount price if the same ad is placed on both Saturday and Sunday, either on the two consecutive days or six days apart.

Press: advertisements and listings

Although many exhibitions open on Mondays and Tuesdays, no one advertises on those days because the *Times* has no regular, assured art columns except on Saturday and Sunday. An ad placed on any other day would be completely lost in the reams of unrelated editorial material. Even if the *Times* carries editorial copy on art during the week, it is useless to ask the advertising department to put an ad on the same page. This is because advertising copy must be designed and made ready earlier than editorial copy, usually before it is yet known whether or not there will be any art news material. Shows, therefore, are usually advertised on the Sunday prior to the opening, with perhaps a tie-in repeat ad on the Saturday following the opening.

The pattern followed by newspapers which cover art events in other cities is easily determined from the individual advertising department. A list of these American papers, with the names of their art critics, can be found in the Appendix to the American Federation of Art's *American Art Directory,* a reference book that is revised and reissued every three years; this directory is not hard to find in libraries and museums. Newspapers which have no art critics often cover art events and shows as features, perhaps on the women's page.

The major monthly art magazines, *Art News* and *Arts,* have national distribution, although their sales are heaviest in the New York area. Shows and the publicity for them must be planned well in advance, for ads must be sent to these monthly publications about four weeks before their publication dates.

The opinons of New York dealers vary considerably regarding the value of advertising in art magazines. Many galleries have annual contracts to advertise in every issue at a discount rate; some don't use the monthlies at all; one well-known New York dealer places small ads regularly—not, he says, because he thinks they bring him any results, but because we have so few art publications in this country that he thinks they should be supported.

American Artist has the largest circulation in the United States among monthly art magazines, but this publication is designed to be technically informative to beginning artists: it does not review gallery shows; therefore ads for exhibitions would not reach the right audience. *Art International* is published in English in Switzerland, but covers much United States art news and has a good percentage of its circulation here; it is used as an advertising medium by numerous dealers, particularly in New York.

The big weeklies like *Time, Life, Look, Newsweek, Cue,* and *The New Yorker,* are not frequently used for gallery ads, first because they are just too expensive, and then because their readership is not primarily interested in contemporary fine arts. Moreover, there is no assurance that an art ad will appear on the art page; it may just get "lost" somewhere in an irrelevant section. Some local weeklies in New

York which carry regular art columns and reviews, and which offer reasonable advertising rates, are more frequently patronized by galleries. Examples of such publications include *New York, Village Voice, Park East,* and on Long Island, *Newsday.*

Many publications list current exhibitions and announce shows about to open. This information is considered editorial copy and therefore costs nothing. Naturally, editors may select what they will list; there is no assurance of complete listing of all galleries. *The New Yorker's* listings, for example, may appear only if the art editor approves.

But in all too many instances a gallery listing is omitted only because the dealer did not get his information to the publication before the deadline. Yet this is a useful form of free publicity and is used as a guide by many readers. Some of these publications are the Sunday *Times* (where listing information must reach the paper even earlier than advertisement information), *The New Yorker, Cue, New York, Arts, Art News.*

Gallery guides

In a number of cities such as New York, Los Angeles, and Louisville, where there are numerous galleries, a monthly booklet is published, listing galleries, giving their addresses and phone numbers, announcing the shows they will have during the month ahead, and specifying the days and hours of visiting. Usually the galleries must pay for these listings. In return, they receive a number of free copies to hand out, or to sell, to their visitors.

These booklets also carry advertisements, as well as reproductions and some editorial copy. A gallery which pays for a listing should send along with its information copy a couple of photographs of work by its exhibiting artists. A reproduction may well be used editorially if it is on hand when layouts are being made for these pocket-sized booklets. If the gallery decides to take not only a listing, but also an advertisement, the publishers are practically certain to use a reproduction in the editorial part of the magazine.

Press releases

A simple, factual, directly written press release can often be helpful to art reviewers and reporters, and hence helpful to the artist in gaining their attention. The kinds to avoid are the flowery, emotional, exaggerated, or introspectively philosophical verbosities that too often emanate from the inexperienced or the egotistical. Press people, who have neither the time nor the patience for such flights of fancy, tend to file them in the waste basket.

The old newsman's 4-W rule, that who, what, where, and when must appear in the first sentence, is a good one. With all the releases that cross my desk, I become irritated when I have to search through numerous paragraphs to discover the opening date of a show, or to find what, in essence, is to be exhibited. Although it should be succinct, it does no harm in the first paragraph to repeat the name and address of the exhibiting gallery, even though these probably also appear in the letterhead above. The reader's eye often goes directly to the body of the text, failing to encompass the larger type at the top. This observaion reminds me of the well-known map publishing firm which issued a huge map of the United States, for which dozens of girls checked the spelling of every little village. When the map came from the press, UNTIED STATES was printed in huge letters across the whole thing: the type was so large that no one saw it.

Using the straight facts, try to write a paragraph or two that describe the art to be shown in a manner which will help to visualize it. When a new reviewer is hired by *Art News,* its editor wisely explains the following approach: think and write as if the reader would never actually see the works of art, so that the words convey the image. Some artists are themselves the ones best able to describe their work; quotations from their statements may well be pertinent. The press likes to use direct quotations because quotes give the impression of having come from the "horse's mouth" (and they fill space without effort or thought).

In a press release you are addressing people who presumably have some knowledge of the field and who can thus comprehend art references. Don't hesitate to make comparisons to other artists and their work if these references will help in visualization. There is nothing pejorative about implying that work stems from, say, Matisse or Shahn or Pollack. All serious artists have derived from their predecessors.

If the exhibiting artist has already been discussed in press notices and reviews, include some quotations from these clippings, advantageously selecting the best, most favorable comments on his work.

The last paragraph of a press release is a good place to give a brief sketch of the artist's professional background: where and with whom he studied; where and when he has exhibited; what collections own examples of his work—especially public collections, but also private ones if they are of importance. Biographical details other than those relating to art background are usually superfluous, unless they relate in some way to the artist's point of view as expressed in his work, or are needed to explain a gap in the continuity of his art production. The biography is sometimes set up in single-spaced copy while the rest of the release is double spaced. This tends to set it apart visually, an aid to the reader pressed for time. It also on occasion saves expenditure, for the single spacing may eliminate the need to run onto an additional page at added cost in mimeographing or multilithing.

If there really is a lot to say and it is expressed in an attention-holding way, there is no harm in a release that is three or four pages long. But if the material can be stated adequately and interestingly in one page, don't drag it out with padding.

Since reproductions are often important to the press, it is advisable to state at the end of the release: PHOTOGRAPHS AVAILABLE, with the telephone number of the gallery where they may be obtained.

It pays to proofread stencils or copy prepared by a printer for mimeographing or multilithing, before it is printed. Typographical errors are generally all too common; when a typist is confronted with technical terms or words totally new and unfamiliar to her, there is no telling how she will mutilate them. *Collage* is almost certain to come out as *college*, and it would seem that most typists are congenitally unable to spell words like *acrylic* and *asymmetric*, even when they are reading accurate copy. This kind of error gives a sloppy, non-professional mien to your show and may influence the reader to think that the whole affair is pretty amateurish.

It is occasionally possible to find a publicity agent specializing in the field of art who knows how to write a good press release and who also maintains an up-to-date press mailing list. But this is rare—and it means an additional cost. Most releases are written by the dealer, and sometimes by the artist, if he has a flair for writing. Results are apt to be more sincere, more accurate, and more effective than those achieved by a hired P.R. hack who knows little or nothing of art and who uses the same sensational approach for everything, whether the subject is art, soap, or racing cars. Most dealers maintain their own mailing lists of press, museum personnel, and customers.

How to use a press release

Editors of the art monthlies, art reviewers for weeklies, and art critics of local daily papers should receive copies of the press release. It is also advantageous to reach editors and writers who work for general periodicals which only occasionally include features on art subjects. You never know when the material you send them may fit in with the theme of some special article they are contemplating. Once you have already ordered the stencils or plates for printing the release, it costs only the small amount for the additional paper to have more copies run off to mail to such feature writers and editors.

If you can write covering letters pointing out the particular feature possibilities of your show, so much the better. Many women artists have thus received coverage on women's pages and in women's magazines. Works of art with a particular slant or theme—whether political, ethnic, technological, or musical—have aroused interest from writers on related subjects.

Curators and directors of local museums which show contemporary art should also be on the mailing list, and some dealers like to mail the release to their customers. Artists often send copies to previous purchasers, perhaps along with an invitation to the preview on which is written something banal but personal, like "Hope you can come." Architects, decorators, and designers may be in a position to influence their clients towards purchasing and commissioning contemporary art. As this trend has grown, more and more dealers and artists have built up their mailing lists to include such professionals, who have become important intermediaries. Indeed, in New York a number of dealers cater especially to this trade, which by itself can supply them with good business.

Many dealers order fifty to a hundred extra copies of the press release to hand out in the gallery, not only to visiting press, but to anyone who shows an interest in the artist's work and wishes information about him.

Mailing houses—often combined with mimeograph and multilith operations—are widely used as expeditors for releases, invitations, brochures, and catalogs (though a good many small galleries address their own mailings by hand). The mailing houses generally operate by machine, putting the list on addressograph plates which are run off automatically onto the envelopes. They can easily separate the lists under different headings, such as: press, museums, architects, customers, in case the dealer wishes to use different sections of his list for different shows. It is important to notify the mailers of any changes in names and addresses and to keep the list up to date. Mailing houses will also address by hand from a special list used so seldom that it is not worth putting onto plates.

Along with the release, it is helpful to send a couple of photographs of the artist's work to a few hand-picked publications such as the art monthlies and the dailies which use art reproductions. Such photographs should have a glossy finish so they can be reproduced; standard sizes are usually 5″ × 7″ or 8″ × 10″. If feasible, send one horizontal picture and one vertical, for the publication then has a better chance to fit one or the other into the layout (the space may permit either a one-column or a two-column cut).

Give the critics as much convincing material as possible, but don't badger them with visits and phone calls. Some artists and dealers have made themselves the *bêtes-noirs* of local critics by constantly pestering them, with the inevitable result that the critics want to stay as far away as possible.

Personal publicity

Sometimes artists who are looking for gallery representation ask me how they can get personal publicity; if they could obtain press coverage, they reason, they would then find a gallery. Actually this is a cart-before-horse approach. To send out a release or other promotion piece without any newspeg such as a forthcoming exhibition, is apt to be a complete waste of time and money. Once in a great while an artist can attract press notice by falling through a window, or by painting while standing on his head. But most of the time the press is too busy to notice; moreover, such feats are unlikely to induce purchases by museums or serious collectors or, in the long run, to build up a professional reputation for the artist.

Brochures, catalogs, invitations

Announcements of exhibitions range all the way from a simple postcard to a book full of color reproductions, with many imaginative variations and eye-catchers among them. A good deal of ingenuity and inventiveness go into some announcements, frequently designed by the artists in keeping with their work. New materials, new printing techniques, and new formats are constantly popping up among these mailing pieces which, when they are truly imaginative, achieve the aim of being noticed and posted—sometimes even becoming collectors' items. The most expensive product is by no means necessarily the most appealing, effective, or attention-getting.

Brochures usually include a brief biographical outline of the artist, often digested from the press release; a check-list of work to be exhibited; and perhaps a quotation or two from an art writer or a previous press notice. However, if the mailing piece is a poster or similar format that limits the space for text, a mimeographed check-list and biography may be folded in with it or handed out at the show.

Galleries which publish catalogs with color reproductions often arrange to have the four-color plates made by engraving firms abroad. Not only is the craftsmanship likely to be of high calibre, but it will be considerably cheaper than similar work done in the United States. If color plates are made, a dealer may subsequently be able to use them for additional publicity by offering them, or electros made from them, to art publications. Such an arrangement is sometimes worked out in advance between a dealer and an editor so that size of color reproduction and time of delivery of plates will suit the needs of both. Obviously, this kind of publicity takes careful advance planning, and is not achieved by the last-minute rush into print which is all too typical of many publicity efforts.

Some dealers with a long-range view put out a periodic bulletin about their artists: where they have exhibited, sold, or been commissioned, and other facts relevant to their recent biographies. These bulletins are not primarily produced to obtain immediate press notice, but the information they contain is likely to go into the morgues of various publications, to be drawn upon at a later, more appropriate time. Bulletins are sent not only to the press, but also to collectors of the artists' works, to keep them and their interest in the artists informed and ever alert.

There are various theories about when to mail announcements and brochures. One of the most common is that they should be posted six or eight days before the opening: the recipient should then have sufficient notice to attend, but not enough time to forget about it; and possible Post Office delays would still not make delivery too late. Another practice is to send notices only one or two days ahead, which I suspect is more a practice than a policy, based on insufficient advance planning rather than on any tenable theory. Many of these arrive the day after the opening.

Radio and television

It is pretty difficult to arouse interest in gallery showings from the big commercial radio and television stations. Although they must carry some cultural-educational material, they are more inclined to cover big museum shows to fulfill this requirement. Many stations do, however, give listings of forthcoming events in the arts; and it is indeed worthwhile to see that these programmers receive notices of gallery exhibitions.

Educational television, now so much on the rise, does offer good potentialities. These channels should certainly be on regular mailing lists; they should also receive photographs, preferably 8″ × 10″, and dull finished (not glossy) so they do not reflect the high-powered lights. These stations are much more likely to give illustrated spot announcements of forthcoming shows than are the commercial channels.

The educational channels, like the commercial ones, are more inclined to emphasize in feature coverage the activities of museums. However, the museums themselves are always looking for interesting material to supply. A good artist who is also an able speaker in interview and discussion situations or who is adept at demonstrations is a boon to this kind of program and should be brought to the attention not only of the educational channel, but also of the museum's publicity department. Also in constant demand are good ideas for television shows that have action, dialogue, and controversy, accompanied by telegenic original material. If the station does not have the funds to send out cameras and crews for shooting on location, then it becomes important to select material which can be transported to the studio.

An artist's chances of obtaining television time are greater if his work can be tied in with a public institution. The channel likes this stamp of authority, which removes from its personnel the onus of making selections in a field they may not know well, and of seeming to "play favorites" among artists and their galleries. Of course, the museum is concerned about its own reputation for good judgment; it is not likely, then, to sponsor the television appearance of artists whose work it deems unworthy of hanging on its walls. In addition, you should consider—before proposing shows to museum publicity directors—that it takes a surprisingly large amount of material to make a decent television presentation. One good "idea" can sometimes be completely exhausted in fifty seconds. A lot of visual and verbal material, and a great deal of thought, must be stacked into even a 10-minute program.

Speeches, demonstrations, happenings

Publicity build-up for an artist is often achieved not only by radio and television appearances, but also through lectures and demonstrations at art schools, clubs, and other organizations. The artist who proves himself able and interesting in making public appearances of this kind is likely to be offered opportunities to become better known. Museums which operate art schools are frequently happy to schedule such events for utilizing the talents of local artists for their students, adult or juvenile. Programs of this nature are also organized for museum members. State and regional art associations (listed with the names of their officers in the *American Art Directory*), and the many art—literary—culture clubs which have latched onto modern art as "in" are also susceptible. Most of these organizations pay artists at least a small honorarium for such services.

An old technique used for attracting notice is the stunt that shocks—a tactic probably stemming from the Dadaists of the 1917-1920 period. The "events" and "happenings" of the 1960s have quite frankly been called "neo-Dada," and in some instances have achieved as much attention as did the toilet-seat the Dadaists once hung as a work of art. Whether the defecations at New York's Judson Church Gallery and the nudist activities in the East Village will go down in art history remains to be seen. Some of these stunts have been based on genuine "reform" motives and aims—as was the Dada movement, in the opinion of many art historians. Others are devised purely as quick attention-getters, without regard to any "cause" or long-term effect. These unconventional art events vary widely in their purposes, methods, sincerity, and, accordingly, in their impact. If they produce only an amused raised eyebrow as a response to their purposeless sensationalism, such tactics may downgrade the participating artists' reputations. On the other hand, sensationalism has indeed been employed to focus attention on conditions too long ignored.

As an example of a publicity announcement aimed at getting the most mileage from the least expensive mimeographed statement (no photographs), the following is good press release writing—whatever you or I think about its content and implication:

"Kusama, High Priestess of Polka Dots, pioneer of naked happenings, and her revolutionary International Society for Self-Obliteration will present a Naked Happening at Fillmore East, Friday and Saturday at 7:30 and 11:00 p.m. The performance will feature Kusama's Beautiful People— NAKED BOYS AND GIRLS—with audience participation." She goes on to promise views of her "Aggregation Furniture: sofas, beds, chairs covered with a seemingly endless growth of sensually soft phallic symbols, made from cloth on a sewing machine." Notice what the "High Priestess" has packed into her first 4-W sentence!

8

Co-operative galleries

For many years, groups of artists have been setting up their own galleries on a co-operative basis. They own the gallery; they also rent space, make decisions jointly, and frequently elect officers and perhaps a board of directors empowered to make certain decisions without having to assemble or poll the entire group.

How they operate

Originally, the artists in a co-op were likely to operate their galleries themselves, pitching in to paint walls, arrange lighting fixtures, install shows and take turns "baby-sitting" the premises. Since these business responsibilities took much time away from the artists' creative work, many co-ops arranged to hire a manager to assume these duties. In this type of arrangement, the member-artists remain the "bosses"; it is they who usually determine, by vote, whom they will take in when they have an opening in their roster.

Like the dealer-gallery, the co-op cannot handle more than about two dozen artists if it is to give each a one-man show approximately every other year, with occasional group shows during the season. An artist seeking to join a co-op must expect to leave his slides with the manager for two or three days so that they can be circulated among all the member-artists for their votes.

Their stylistic direction

Co-ops are frequently less dedicated to one particular direction than dealer-galleries, sometimes even purposely seeking diversification in styles, as long as the work in question seems strong. By contrast, artists with similar leanings have been known to band together in co-ops, particularly (as with abstract-expressionism) if their style was waning in popularity, making it more difficult for them to find other exposure and outlets for their work. Even so, such groups have often accepted new recruits of other persuasions.

Not all co-op shows are limited to the work of members. Some groups vary their presentations, including an occasional benefit exhibition or theme show of work by other artists if the causes and purposes appeal to the co-op group. These non-membership shows not only lend variety, but sometimes help to publicize the gallery, and sometimes bring in revenue, when, for example, benefit organizations pay rent for the space.

Costs of operation

The costs of operation are shared by member-artists on one basis or another. In some typical New York cases, each artist pays a monthly fee of $25 to $30; this amount may be less if the gallery is located in a low-rent area. In addition, the artists pay a 25% commission on sales instead of the usual 40%. From these funds come both the rent and the manager's salary. Publicity costs are paid by each artist when his work is being publicized, as in most dealer-galleries. However, the co-op artist is permitted more freedom to determine what kind of brochure and advertising he wants and how much to spend.

Another method of cost-sharing is to require a flat initial membership fee of, say, $100 with no monthly stipend; in addition, each artist pays the manager's salary for the three-week period of his own one-man show; and the co-op takes only a 10% commission on sales.

Financial and other advantages

Although some artists regard the co-op only as a stepping-stone to affiliation with a dealer, many others genuinely prefer this method of exposure. They have more control over their own shows, and more influence over who will be their companion artists in the gallery. Moreover, if an artist's work sells well, he makes more in the co-op, for the lower commission rate more than offsets the relatively small fees paid by the artist-owners. In some cases, artists have left co-ops to join dealer-galleries only to return after a couple of years for the better income.

Special artist galleries

A few galleries in New York have been organized by groups of artists who are already affiliated with regular dealer-galleries. Their purposes are to further the exposure and sale of work by already recognized artists who have more material than their dealer-galleries can handle; the double affiliation is made with the complete agreement of the contract gallery. Usually, the work shown is multiple material such as prints, additional examples from sculpture series, or multiples of mixed-media assemblages and three-dimensional molded or pressed forms. Sometimes these special artist-galleries simply handle small-sized paintings, for many dealer-galleries don't want to bother with small works which don't produce enough revenue to pay for their more expensive display quarters.

The Sculptors' Guild, in New York, which accepts as members only affiliated artists, and which has its own gallery to show members' work regularly, also organizes annual exhibitions at popular show places such as Lever House, outdoor shows in Bryant Park (with sculptor demonstrations in tents), and other activities that attract additional audiences, publicity, and sales for its artists. It also occasionally introduces groups of new, non-member sculptors previously unknown in New York. It is a form of co-op gallery, but one limited to artists who also have dealer-galleries representing them. New members must be proposed and voted on by those who are already members. These "extra" galleries can be very useful to you if you are able to qualify.

9

Artist groups
and
organizations

The *American Art Directory* lists some 500 United States art organizations, and no one knows how many informally organized art groups—the ones that frequently spring up and sometimes vanish—may exist. The more permanent national organizations have been published in a "Directory of National Art Organizations," (1969, $2) by the Associated Councils of the Arts, 1564 Braodway, New York, N.Y. 10036; it gives detailed information on twenty-seven major organizations and lists many others.

Where can you go to talk art?

There are about 600 art schools in the country. Periodically such institutions arrange public discussions and display work by faculty and students, outlets that provide some measure of exposure for artists and the opportunity to meet and exchange ideas. We in this country lack one of the most charming and conducive systems of communication, so common in Europe. We do not have the café or coffee house habit, the designated meeting place where artists can drop by on a particular day of the week, knowing they will find other artists of more or less their persuasions and interests with whom they can engage in stimulating conversation and discussion.

Many artists new to New York have asked me, "How can I get to know some other artists here? Where can we talk art? What artists' organizations are there?" I can only deplore the absence of this old European rendez-vous arrangement and wonder why we have never developed it. Perhaps it is because we have the barbarous (to Europeans) habit of rushing home to a six o'clock dinner, thus leaving ourselves no free time in the early evening for *l'heure de l'apéritif*. Perhaps it is due to our insistence on being efficient, on inflexibly plotting by calendar each hour of the day. Perhaps Americans are more geared to spending all spare time with spouses. Whatever the reason, our artists are missing out on a rewarding experience, one which has engendered many group activities and many stimulating individual developments abroad. Some years ago I worked with a number of Europe-oriented New York artists to establish an *heure de l'apéritif* rendez-vous near the Museum of Modern Art. First we found that though they were theoretically interested, artists were running to catch the next bus home. Then the restaurant, whose back room we had been able to commandeer once a week, folded up! Perhaps some American artists can make a more successful arrangement in a less harried city than New York.

The Club

New York does have something known just as "The Club," loosely organized a good number of years ago as a kind of abstract-expressionist group. It was frequently attended by Willem de Kooning, its unofficial monitor and leader. The Club has undergone mutations both in attendance and ideology, but during the art season it still meets on Friday nights—*after* supper—in various downtown New York halls. Sometimes The Club convenes just for discussion with coffee or beer; other times it offers a program and speaker. This information will not help an artist who does not yet know other artists in New York. Non-member admission to these sessions is by invitation of a member only.

Judson Church Gallery and other meeting places

Another occasional gathering place in New York is the gallery of the Judson Church on Washington Square South, where the avant-garde has one of its centers. More often, however, artists assemble in one anothers' studios for discussion and exchange of ideas.

Existing art organizations have many functions; some provide an opportunity to mingle with other artists. Many are not hard to join if your interests are similar. Annual dues are not high—generally from $8 to $15 a year. In many cases artists who are already members vote on the new applicants, usually after viewing their work and their records (frequently no formidable ordeal).

The American Art Directory

There are organizations specializing in just about everything: for work by veterans, the American Veterans' Society of Artists, Inc; for watercolors, the American Watercolor Society; for work by women, the National Association of Women Artists, the Pen and Brush Club (New York only), and the Catherine Lorillard Wolfe Art Club (New York only); for sculpture, the National Sculpture Society; for murals, the National Society of Mural Painters; for casein painting, the National Society of Painters in Casein; and for work related to the performing arts, the Library and Museum of the Performing Arts, Lincoln Center, New York.

All these organizations, plus many others, can be found in the *American Art Directory*. Because this directory appears only every three years, the new organizations constantly developing are, perforce, not included. Moreover, the officer listings for art organizations, museums, and art schools lag far behind personnel changes. It is a pity that supplements are not published at least annually to list additions and changes, as is the practice of the *Art Index*, the standard guide to art periodicals. This valuable reference issues paperback supplements every few months.

Specialized and general organizations

A new development in the field of intermedia, for example, must wait a couple of years before it is noted in the directory. This time lag makes it difficult for artists to locate multi-media centers that require a variety of talents working together. In the meantime, artists and film makers involved in developing the light or illumination arts have formed USCO; and collaborating artists and scientists have set up E.A.T. (Experiments in Art and Technology), with various branches around the country.

There are many art organizations listed in the directory which have no particular specialization: Allied Artists of America; American Society of Contemporary Artists; Audubon Artists (which has nothing to do with pictures of birds, as some artists have believed and have therefore avoided the various activities of the group); Knickerbocker Artists; National Arts Club; and Kappa Pi, the international honorary art fraternity with chapters in colleges, universities, and art schools throughout the United States. Most of these organizations periodically exhibit their members' work and also select for showing, either by jury or membership vote, work submitted by non-members. Many organizations which do not have adequate exhibition space themselves arrange to use the galleries of organizations such as New York's National Academy, Riverside Museum, Lever House Gallery, or IBM Gallery. Organizations with these facilities usually make them available only to acceptable groups to use for exhibition purposes. As an individual, it would be pointless for you to apply for such space.

Business Committee for the Arts

A Business Committee for the Arts was established in 1967 under the aegis of David Rockefeller, with Douglas Dillon as Chairman. Its expressed purpose is "to stimulate, encourage, and advise" in the fields of both the visual and the performing arts. From ninety corporate leaders as charter members, they raised $825,000. The Committee does not itself administer the funds. Rather, it acts as broker between corporations and various art groups, for purchases and commissions. Hopefully, this organization will eventually increase corporations' interest and involvement in the arts. (In 1965, the total corporate contribution to health, education, welfare, and culture amounted to $700 million; of this sum the arts received only .028%, or $19 million.) It may prove useful to art groups to register with this Committee, whose headquarters are located at 1270 Avenue of the Americas, New York, N.Y. 10020.

Local and regional organizations

There are also many local and regional organizations throughout the country. Some are connected with a museum, as, for example, the Birmingham Art Association, which puts on an annual juried show at the Birmingham Museum of Art, holds annual non-juried shows for members, and sponsors each October the Alabama State Fair Art Exhibition. Some art associations and leagues, in areas where no museum exists, help to fill the gap by holding regular exhibitions, competitions with awards, clothesline shows, lectures, classes, and sketch nights. Community art associations frequently utilize local libraries as their show places. Regional groups also exist in most parts of the country. For example, the Pacific Northwest Arts and Crafts Association in Bellevue, Washington exhibits regional work—all for sale —in juried and open shows, with awards and with purchases that are subsequently circulated to schools and municipal centers in the region. University and art school galleries sometimes serve as centers for regional exhibitions.

Ethnic and national group organizations

Certain organizations are established for particular ethnic or national groups. For example, Indian artists periodically show in various museums and galleries in collaboration with the Bureau of Indian Affairs. Black artists exhibit at the Harlem Studio Museum, Harlem's Schomburg branch of the New York Public Library, and the North Carolina College Museum, in Durham. Artists and craftsmen from remote countries of the world can be seen at Carnegie Peace

Building and at the Institute of International Education Building, both located at United Nations Plaza in New York City; and at Columbia University's International House. Jewish artists show at the Gallery of Israeli Art, and at Hertzl Institute, both in Manhattan. The work of Latin-American and Canadian artists is the specialty of the Center for Inter-American Relations, in New York City.

Artists from foreign countries

Artists from a foreign country should visit their consulate in New York or their embassy in Washington, where an attaché concerned with cultural affairs should be able to direct them to special outlets. (I say "should be able" advisedly, for not infrequently attachés refer artists to the Art Information Center, which is all right, too.) Centers sponsored by foreign governments and certain dealer-galleries specialize in showing contemporary work from particular countries: in New York special exhibitions can be seen of work by artists from Haiti, China, Japan, Armenia, Czechoslovakia, Austria, Puerto Rico, and Latin America. There is even a gallery that shows comtemporary Persian miniatures! The airlines of Australia, France, Portugal, and Scandinavia have nobly gotten into the act, setting aside good viewing areas in their show places for work by contemporary artists from their countries.

Artists' Equity

Artists' Equity, originally set up in 1947, is a unique artist organization—the closest thing there is to an artists' union. It was established to promote and protect the economic welfare of professional artists. No one can join until he has had at least one, one-man exhibition. Artists' Equity is a national organization with seventeen chapters throughout the country. The local chapters have no great interrelation, although the National Board of Directors, which is empowered to determine national policies and programs, is officially composed of the chapter presidents. (See Appendix for list of chapters and their officers.)

Though originally in New York, the organization's national headquarters has for some years now been located at 229 Broadway East, Seattle, Washington 98102. When the move was made, the New York chapter's activities at first considerably dropped off, then the chapter was reconstituted with renewed vigor. The New Yorkers (currently disenchanted with Seattle Headquarters and independent of it) found office space with an exhibition area for group shows of members' works of art. They have worked with New York's Attorney General on the recently enacted state law protecting artists against absconding and fraud, as well as on other pertinent legislation such as that requiring the allocation of a percentage of public building funds for art work and commissions. In addition, the New York Artists' Equity investigates studio and housing potentials for artists; publicizes information in the members' newsletters that may help artists to obtain fellowships or grants; and announces forthcoming competitive exhibitions that they may enter. It also arranges member discounts on art materials and art magazine subscriptions; offers group rates for health insurance; scouts around for banks and other public buildings where it can mount exhibitions of members' work: and informs artists about legal aspects of wills and taxes involving artists' works.

Similar activities are carried on by some other local chapters. If the chapter in your area is not very active, its structural framework might be worth preserving and implementing to make the chapter more useful. Artists' Equity is an organization that is likely to endure—despite its many past and current upheavals and disagreements—for its basic premises and goals are more oriented toward preserving and expanding artists' rights than those of any other organization in the profession.

10

Exhibiting without gallery or group affiliation

If you have not yet had any showings—and even if you have had some—you may need to build up your art background and experience before any recognized dealer will take you on. It helps a dealer when he can say to a vacillating customer that your work has been selected by some well-known jury, juror, or institution. If he has to admit you have never shown anywhere, his sales job is more difficult.

Juried exhibitions and competitive shows

One way to make your art background more impressive is through open competitive shows. A really good dealer in a major art center will submit your work for you; but if you do not have this kind of conscientious dealer behind you, it is your job to enter the work yourself.

I recently received a letter from an artist in Lima, Peru, asking me to send him the addresses of organizations that hold competitive and group exhibitions. Indeed, this is the kind of information which artists *anywhere* would like to have at their fingertips. Currently, there is not even one reliable annual reference that lists the numerous juried and competitive shows which regularly take place around the country. Artists' Equity used to mimeograph and publish such a list for the ensuing year. Quite logically, the organization gave it up because the participating institutions kept changing the dates of their shows after publication, thus rendering the list relatively useless. The best you can do at this time to inform yourself about juried exhibitions and competitive shows is to consult the monthly art magazines, read Artists' Equity Newsletters (where local chapters publish them), and pay attention to announcements posted on bulletin boards of art schools and of university and college art departments.

Art News, for example, gives monthly listings under the heading "Where and When To Exhibit." Here, in fine print, you can find the forthcoming exhibitions to be held in various parts of the country, with details about how to enter. *Art News* is a nationally distributed magazine and should be easy to find in libraries. Consult it the first of each month, right after it appears. This practice is advisable because some listings require you to apply for entry blanks by the eighth or tenth of the month. There is usually a small entry fee for handling—around $3.00. In many cases, you are first asked to send 35 mm. color slides for viewing; those which prove to be of interest may be marked and returned to you with a request that you send the originals for final decision by the jury.

Annuals and biennials

There are numerous annuals and biennials around the United States which are well worth trying to enter. Some, like those of New York's National Academy and the Audubon Society, and Philadelphia's Pennsylvania Academy of the Fine Arts, are located in art metropolises. Others, such as the Butler Institute of American Art in Youngstown, Ohio, and the University of Southern Illinois in Carbondale, may seem rather remote from major centers of art purchasers, dealers, and critics. Don't turn up your nose at them because of their geographic location. They have good juries; they publish well illustrated catalogues which get around to dealers, museums and critics; and they have purchase prizes. Inclusion in such shows will certainly help build up your reputation.

Jurors

Not all competitive shows are worth entering, however. You can learn something about their caliber from the entry blanks, obtainable free on request, which spell out terms and purposes, and usually list names of jurors. If they don't list the jurors, write and ask. If you don't know who the jurors are, look them up in *Who's Who* or *Who's Who in American Art*. Usually, though, a jury listing will include each juror's credentials.

A well-known juror can make all the difference between a show worth entering and just a nice local art activity, without any broader value. Some local and regional art groups are sufficiently enterprising and far sighted to obtain top-notch jurors for their annuals, which, though limited to artists from the area, often are not limited to their own members only. The West Virginia Art Association, for example, has persuaded Lloyd Goodrich, for many years Director of the Whitney Museum, and Brian O'Doherty, art author and formerly of *The New York Times* Art Department, to journey to Charleston as jurors. Even such busy and prominent men like to gain an insight into the art activities taking place in various parts of the country. The advantage to the participating artists is obvious, since they can say their work was selected by a well-known juror. Moreover, local press, radio, and television give more complete coverage to the shows because of the visiting expert.

To enhance the importance of their shows in this way, members of local or regional art associations must be willing to put up the funds for a round-trip ticket and a modest honorarium—perhaps $100. ("Honorarium" is the polite term for a sum insufficient to be called a fee for the services rendered.) The visiting juror is usually entertained for two or three days in a private home; he may appear on television and radio; he may give a talk at the local museum or to the association's members while he is in town. Once an association has obtained a noted juror, it paves the way and makes it easier for that organization to persuade other potential jurors in ensuing years.

Some of the competitive shows conducted by institutions and organizations are aimed at only one style of art. This style may not at all be in your vein, and hence it would be futile for you to attempt to participate. You can usually judge its suitability by the entry form's description of the exhibition aims and the type of juror engaged. On the other hand, don't be misled by a name such as "National Academy" into believing its shows will include only old-fashioned academicians. Actually, the Academy's shows include all styles and directions.

Watch out for the kind of competitive show whose aim, if you read between the lines, is purely to enhance the public relations image of the sponsoring organization. Some hotels, for example, have advertised "competitive" shows to be exhibited in the lobby. They often "fudge" about who is to make the selections, using vague cover-up phrases like "juried by noted art experts"—experts who never materialize. They offer some prizes—and charge the artists enough per entry to pay for them. Such exploitative competitions are likely to accept all submitted works, without selection, as long as payment is received. Its promulgators hope for hotel publicity by getting on the art band wagon, aiming to maneuver the show so that you, the artist, will pay for it without benefit to yourself. Shows like these are not covered by prominent critics or museum curators. Instead of adding to your art background, they just drain your pocketbook.

Department store galleries

Department stores are becoming increasingly involved in contemporary art, many having established separate areas for galleries within their precincts, with art dealers to direct them. Though by no means a new departure, this activity is definitely becoming more widespread. A few department store galleries, such as Gump's in San Francisco and J.L. Hudson in Detroit, are generally accepted in the same category as other professional galleries in town.

So far, however, the majority of these galleries have not

"made the grade" professionally. A kind of snob rejection still prevails. But time, as well as careful selection and operation, will probably break down opposition. There is, indeed, a substantial argument in favor of these outlets, which offer something of a captive audience and which do not intimidate the young or new purchaser who is apt to think—quite incorrectly—that if he even walks into an art gallery he won't escape without shelling out a sizable sum. He (or more often she, in this case) feels more at ease in a department store, where he knows his way around and understands how, if need be, to apply sales resistance.

A number of department stores have started galleries which emphasize "safe" work by big names—often in the less expensive graphic media. In some instances, the examples are dubious; they may be lithographic reproductions of original lithographs by, say, Toulouse-Lautrec, misleadingly advertised as lithographs by the master. The eminent Print Council of America tries valiantly to thwart this practice. A pamphlet defining a truly "original" print is available from the Council, but too few purchasers are aware of this source of information, and too many are taken in by misleading labels and ads. This dubious practice, only occasionally found in department stores, is, unfortunately, not hard to find elsewhere. (See Appendix for Print Council definitions and distinctions.)

Gradually, department store galleries are demonstrating more courage about taking work by newer, less-known artists. Their approach and quality, of course, depend upon the caliber of the gallery director and on the degree of independent judgment he is allowed by his employers. As attitudes become more enlightened, department stores may become promising outlets, providing contemporary artists with a growing market.

Bookstores

Some bookstores also set aside areas for art galleries. Sometimes they specialize only in original book illustrations. In other instances, they express a genuine interest in contemporary, non-illustration works of art. Within its domain on Fifth Avenue, the old established Brentano's in New York operates the Galerie Moderne, where group and one-man shows—often by younger artists—are a regular feature. In other cities where there are fewer art galleries, bookstores may generate more art activity—not necessarily because they are nobly filling a gap, but perhaps because they are "latching on" to another sales potential. If a good bookstore in your city has not heretofore shown art, you might persuade the owner that it is the coming thing to do so.

Be prepared for the "safe" attitude in some of the big bookstores which do display art—but only by well knowns. An artist who came to see me the other day said she had gone to Rizzoli's, a *de luxe* Italian bookstore in New York which shows and advertises big name art. She was told, she said: "You will only become the two-thousand-and-first on our list of applicants." It is not hard to tell, just by looking around, which firms show only established artists; it may be a bit harder to persuade them to alter their policy.

Banks

With all their dull architecture built from the wealth derived from our pockets, banks have taken over huge street-level areas with great display fronts of plate glass and thermopane. Yet they have nothing to display, which makes walking along the avenues a pretty boring affair. A few banks, having become vaguely aware of their lack of eye appeal, have been willing to use their great picture windows for art—even, occasionally, for a pretty female artist actually painting on the spot. A new and fancy branch of a savings bank recently opened in my neighborhood with more street-front display windows than any ten New York galleries put together. There sat a young lady painting, gawked at by mobs, all kinds of people on the sidewalk, from the soup kitchen line of the nearby charity house to the brokers of the nearby stock exchange house. After the opening weeks, no more art appeared.

Obviously it is going to take enterprise and boosting on the part of artists if they wish to jolt these firms out of their familiar and comfortable ruts, but it has been and can be done. Individual artists and groups, such as New York's Artists' Equity, have more often engendered such activities in banks than have the banks' own personnel. Even though this kind of display has not yet commanded much professional recognition, the enormous viewing advantages of these showplaces make them potentially prime art display spots. This is what happened at Lever House on Park Avenue, whose directors long ago realized they could not make appealing shows out of acres of their soap, and so gave over their exhibition space to art. Exhibitions at Lever House are recognized professionally and do get reviewed. Besides, they can be seen day and night, for they are lighted after the building closes and are fully visible from the street through the glass walls. The Lever House managers simplify their role as arbiters by accepting work by established groups only; these groups encompass many artists and styles. There is no reason why bank outlets, if intelligently and imaginatively administered, cannot achieve the same status.

Libraries

All over the country libraries are devoting more and more space to contemporary art shows. Again, much has been achieved by artists themselves. A happy example is the public library in a little New England town which I visit on weekends. In recent years, the library's volunteer board of directors was persuaded by one of the directors, herself an artist, to permit her to organize regular shows of contemporary art on the library walls. She has kept the library buzzing ever since with art and artists—some local, some "imported" —with openings and, in good weather, outdoor sculpture on the lawn. Good local publicity and sales have resulted, as well as a new awareness of art on the part of many local residents, some of whom have been inspired to make their first art purchases. Libraries have tax-supported space and a regular audience; generally they simply need some help and know-how to start such an operation. The chances are that most libraries will welcome a practical suggestion and plan of operation.

In big cities, certain branch libraries specialize in art because of their locations; some of them have especially designated art galleries. In New York, for example, there are galleries in the Hudson Branch of the New York Public Library, because it is in Greenwich Village where many artists live, work, or congregate; in the Donnell Branch because it is located across the street from the Museum of Modern Art; and in the Schomburg Branch, which for many years was the only major showing place in Harlem for black artists. Some city libraries put on only group shows; others arrange one-man exhibitions. Such libraries usually have regular opening previews and often sponsor related talks, discussions, lectures, demonstrations, and films. Works are for sale. Not much major publicity attends these shows in large cities, but they do successfully reach neighborhood audiences. Participating in library exhibitions gives you experience—and exposure of your work under any reputable auspices is not to be sneezed at.

Churches

One tends to think that liberal religious sects—such as Universalist, Unitarian, or Community Churches—are those most open to encouraging contemporary art. Indeed, they often are favorably inclined and hospitable to artists; but they don't have a corner on the market. Some of the reputedly "staid" denominations—like the Presbyterians and Episcopalians—have become interested and are mounting shows in their parish houses, auditoriums, or Sunday school rooms. Some of them seek out contemporary work which has a Biblical context. It is occasionally apparent that if the title alone has some religious reference, the church will happily include it, regardless of any evident visual relationship to a religious theme. Perhaps a reverent title suffices to justify the show to a Board.

Church and synagogue interest in modern art has been manifest for many years both here and abroad. They have often led the way, especially in architecture, where church design (perhaps most notably the Catholic and Jewish) has really pioneered and has embraced the arts of stained glass, tapestry, mural painting, sculpture, and altar accessories to embellish their new buildings. Not only have they exhibited, they have purchased and commissioned works of art as well.

In small communities, churches are often interested in showing contemporary art, particularly if they don't have to worry about paying guards and insurance out of small budgets. Actually, the church is probably safer from theft and fire than an artist's home or studio. Again, in my small New England weekend town, I have been asked on several occasions by a local minister about the possibility of showing modern art in his new parish house. He must really be interested, for we never meet in church, but only over a beer in the one local lunch room. Although he has shown many good art reproductions, he has been scared about assuming the responsibility of displaying originals. I suspect that he and many other clergymen in similar positions would happily display work by local artists if these artists offered their encouragement and help in selecting, installing, and protecting the shows.

Furniture stores

Some forward-looking furniture stores which are open to the public (for "trade" outlets, see page 59) make a practice of inviting artists to display work in their showrooms when they feel the art is compatible with their merchandise. Their managers are usually entirely willing to sell the art—often without commission—charging the artist only for such expenses as framing and customer delivery. The works of art and the furniture displays complement one another, and the enlightened manager likes to see his wares thus enhanced. Often these stores change the art about once a month, perhaps showing one painter and one sculptor each month. If you see a handsome display of furniture, with or without concomitant art, it can do no harm to show the store manager reproductions or examples of your work for potential inclusion. Also, the manager with no art in his store may just not know where to get it.

Charity shows and auctions

New York dealers are apt to frown on frequent requests for donations from their artists to large, fancy charitable sales and auctions (see page 48)—and with reason. However, New York artists with no gallery affiliation tell me that contributions to small, out-of-town churches and synagogues and charitable clubs can be worthwhile. The expectations of these organizations are more modest—they usually ask only for 20% to 25% for charitable purposes, which amount is a tax-deductible item on the artist's income. When the charitable sale takes the form of an auction, the artist can insist on placing a minimum bid on his work. In general, this is the only kind of auction that makes sense for the living artist to participate in. The regular auction houses usually sell work by living artists only when it is included in a whole collection or estate, and such auctions are not the concern of the artist. There is a move afoot, however, to try to enact legislation that will enable the artist to receive a royalty on increased prices in subsequent sales over his original price. A few top artists have already achieved such agreements with their dealers; but, of course, such royalty advantages do not extend to auction houses, being limited to resales by the artist's dealer. Even this modest improvement, however, is as yet extremely rare.

Suburban galleries

Some New York artists have also found it profitable to go out of town to suburban galleries. They load up a station wagon with work and cruise around showing it. They find that numerous galleries of this sort are pleased to have work brought to them on consignment; these galleries charge no expenses and generally expect a commission on sales of only 33⅓%, or sometimes even less. It is well to keep in mind that people who buy in the outlying areas are not likely to spend as much as if they were to go into the city for a major purchase. Smaller works and graphics are more suitable than a major opus.

Studio "open house"

Artists who have no gallery commitments sometimes hold "open house" at their studios, usually on weekends or an occasional evening. In New York, several artists in a neighborhood occasionally get together and advertise that they will all have open house on the same day so that the visitor can easily go from one to another on a single trip. Some artists have sold by this device, others have not. Occasionally, they have received good publicity.

The pupils of artists who are teachers are also potential purchasers. They usually want to visit their teacher's studio, and this often results in a sale.

Many artists exchange works with one another. I know one artist who had visitors at his studio open house only to find that one of them preferred his friend's work obtained on "swap." Instead of being insulted, he sold the friend's work. The friend, who had the same privilege of selling the work he had obtained in the swap, was pleased to learn he had another collector. Some artists who are better salesmen than their friends have hung in their studios some work by friends along with their own, and have sold for them on a commission basis.

Thus the artist, without gallery affiliation but with ingenuity, has been able to devise numerous ways of exhibiting and selling. And the old barter system of exchanging art for needed services or materials has long worked for many artists. Doctors and dentists for years have been noted for their willingness to be paid in art—and not just because they have offices and waiting-rooms to decorate (a form of exposure for the artist), for so do lawyers, who are not noted for taking barter payment. Doctors and dentists are sufficiently interested in painting and sculpture to have established numerous art organizations around the country which periodically show their own hobby work. And there is an occasional expert in both fields—such as Herbert Ferber, one of our most noted sculptors who, under another name, is a highly professional dentist.

The medical-artistic affinity may perhaps be explained only by psychiatrists. But the barter trend is spreading into many other fields. An artist recently told me that he had had a carpet laid in his apartment. The man who installed it said, "You painted these pictures? Well, I'd rather have a picture than the money." The artist was indeed surprised, but he claims that a lot of artists practically live on barter. Electricians, plumbers, wall painters, and accountants have been known to take art in lieu of pay.

Open-air shows

All over the country there are "clothesline," village green, or sidewalk exhibitions during good weather. Many of these shows may not amount to anything professionally—they are basically for amateurs—but they may produce sales. Some, on the other hand, are competently juried by professionals and also display invited work by recognized artists. A well organized outdoor show with jurors, such as Boston's annual, puts to shame New York's Washington Square show. The latter is available to anyone who rents sidewalk and fence space—an odd practice since the sidewalks and fences do not belong to those who collect the rent for them. There has been talk for years of making the Washington Square show more like the Boston—perhaps this discussion will one day bear fruit.

It probably won't hurt your reputation to show even in the unjuried outdoor exhibitions. I have known several professional artists newly arrived in New York who unwittingly took their work to Washington Square, and subsequently went on to reputable dealers who did not hold this against them, realizing their naiveté. But there is quite a bit of work and time involved in such shows: you usually have to be personally responsible for everything, including baby-sitting your part of the show. The question you must answer for yourself is, is it worth it? Is it going to add up to something on your art background record? On the other hand, it may be worth while for local recognition in your area, and for revenue from sales.

Museums and lending libraries

If the museums in your area show contemporary art—and many do—their curator of painting and sculpture, or their curator of graphics will usually see work, or slides of work by living artists. It can do no harm to call the curator's office and ask how to arrange for an appointment. Systems in museums vary considerably, so you need to find out what the particular procedure is. The Whitney Museum in New York, for example, has four "viewings" a year, and artists may not apply for a viewing more often than once every two years. If you call or write the museum for an appointment, you will probably not get an answer until about ten days before the appointed time. Then you will receive a card stating the day to appear and stipulating what to bring—probably two or three originals to be left for a few days and then picked up. Don't expect the Whitney or other museums to make comments, judgments, or criticisms of your work. They usually make their own notes, but say nothing. From these viewings the Whitney picks a certain number of works for their annuals. You have nothing to lose except transportation time, and you are at least entered "in their records." Some museums request slides to keep, say, for a week. During this time they are shown to various curators before you return to pick them up.

Even those regional museums which are notoriously old fashioned about exhibiting modern work are more open-minded about showing their own local artists. They manifest an almost forced attitude of community responsibility, and they are more apt to receive newspaper publicity if their "local boy makes good." Museums just love publicity; it pays off well with their trustees and other donors. Consequently, if you are a "local" artist, you might as well cash in on this situation.

Some museums have art lending libraries—often as a special privilege and as a come-on for membership in the museum. People can rent works of art which are for sale, usually applying the rental price onto the sales price if they decide to buy the piece after living with it. The rental period is usually limited to about two months.

At New York's Museum of Modern Art, you cannot be selected to show in the lending library unless you exhibit in a recognized dealer-gallery. This regulation was made because the Museum's "council" of donors wants the feeling of art importance besides their money-donation importance. The Museum allows members of the council to select potential work for rental from professional New York galleries. The Museum is not willing, however, to let the council go to unaffiliated artists' studios. Thus, council members feel they are using their art acumen, while the Museum is assured of a "safer" initial selection for rentals; selections are then subject to final curatorial revision and elimination. All museums have to pander to their donors in one way or another; and the selection process is a form of educational indoctrination for council members which is likely to lead to more purchases of modern art.

There are various systems of making selections for art rentals, both in museums and in some dealer-galleries here and there; it may be worth your while to look into this outlet. The rental fee, however produces little or no profit for the artist, for the amount will probably be absorbed by insurance and administrative costs. Some artists resent this situation, as well as the possibility that if their work is not bought by the renter, a pejorative stamp may be put on it—a kind of "used and rejected" label. Others, however, have found rental libraries useful for exposure and sales.

11

Miscellaneous tips and observations

Geographic location

The most difficult inquiries arriving at the Art Information Center from artists seeking gallery outlets come from those who live in areas geographically so remote from any major art center that I don't know what to suggest. They have usually been referred to the Center by a United States Information Service official or a cultural attaché at the American Embassy, people who didn't know how to fulfill the artists' needs either.

From Ghana I received this note: "Exhibition of Drawings and Paintings: I am a 33-year-old Ghanian (African) lecturer in the Faculty of Art. I am also a practicing painter and have held exhibitions both in Ghana and in London. I paint mostly in oils and gouache—mostly on Ghanian life— working, dancing, worshiping, marketing, etc. I have quite a number of my paintings on slides. . . . Do please let me hear from you as soon as you can. Thanks."

What can I suggest to such a person other than that, since he got once to London, maybe he can develop permanent representation in a gallery there and possibly be "found" by a scouting New York dealer—who is most unlikely to scout in Ghana (although this situation may soon change, now that Africa is the "in" place to travel).

An investment company in Australia wrote: "Our present concern is to explore the possibilities of introducing the work of Australian artists to collectors in New York as part of a scheme of exhibitions. The idea is to find a known, good gallery in each of a number of cities who would be prepared to show our Australian collection perhaps once a year and hold a modest stock for sale at other times, act as a centre for enquiries, etc."

It never even occurred to this firm that a "known, good gallery" would have its roster pretty full and would be able to find other worthy artists much closer by; or to consider all the freight and insurance costs; or to realize that a good dealer naturally wants to see originals before making decisions. And suppose he doesn't like them after they have come all that way? Geographic location, when it is remote, does indeed play a part. I hope you don't live *too* far away!

Paris used to be the art center of the world; now New York is. This fact does not mean that the wisest move is to New York. Many artists have fared better by concentrating on showing regionally, at good galleries in nearby cities. Should their great desire be eventually to get to New York, this procedure is still good, for New York dealers travel frequently in the United States and in Europe to scout for new talent. If they become interested in your work in a local gallery, they are near enough to visit your studio, where they can see more of your work on the spot. How much more practical this procedure is than packing up and coming to New York on an expensive and risky trip! If you are determined to bring your work to Manhattan, first show locally, as much and as widely as possible, to build up reputation before you tackle the world's art center.

In some ways the out-of-town artist has it easier, for exhibiting and receiving recognition is not as difficult outside New York. In the same week, I recently talked to two artists, who proved to be extremes in the two situations. One was a New York girl who had just started painting, but thought she had it made because she lived in the art center of the world. Having painted all of two pictures, she was already looking for a dealer! By way of contrast, an artist who came here from California had spent years showing wherever he could in the West, entering juried shows and winning awards. He had built up a very impressive list of some forty such recognitions before ever approaching the New York market. Needless to say, the Californian found gallery representation; the New Yorker did not.

One useful way to build up your art background before tackling New York is to offer gifts of drawings and prints to local museums. Naturally the curators will not accept them, even as gifts, unless they find the art worthy, but they are more apt to acquiesce if they don't have to strain their limited budgets. If the donations are accepted, you can then legitimately state that your work is "in the collection" of this and that museum. No need to mention that the works are graphics, which are easier to give away and less depleting of your major works which, of course, you would prefer to retain for selling.

Age and sex

Some dealers tend to stress youth in choosing the artists they show. Occasionally, dealers express doubts about the effectiveness and dedication of women artists, because many of them—unlike most men—are supported and need to sacrifice little or nothing to pursue their art activities.

But these are by no means widespread attitudes. Many dealers and critics think in terms of the art, without regard to the physical characteristics of its creators. Nevertheless, matters of age and sex seem to be bugaboos to numerous artists. Some women use only a last name on catalogs and ads for their shows to hide their sex; some middle-aged artists won't list in their catalogs their recognitions and exhibitions of earlier years, for fear of being "dated." Such subterfuges are, of course, likely to be uncovered sooner or later, with consequent loss of respect. Perhaps they are exaggerated.

The New York dealer who seems to be most vocal about his distaste for "suburban housewife artists" (to the point of sounding like a misogynist) nevertheless exhibits work by females whom he considers serious and valid. Perhaps the woman's work has to be better than the man's to make the grade, but women in every field are inured to this as a fact of their lives. Whatever the current fad or prejudice may be, age, experience, know-how, and maturity in many cases interest dealers and critics more than just the flashiness of youth—which may turn out to be just a flash in the pan.

Temperament

Both artists and dealers are widely reputed to be temperamental. Sometimes, dealers may seem more temperamental than artists; perhaps they are frustrated artists who do not have the outlet for self-expression that artists have. But a whimsical, impractical artist can be the bane of existence to a dealer who is efficient and businesslike. The following examples may seem extreme and exaggerated, but they happened not long ago.

A sculptor arranged with a dealer for a show of her work and, after it was installed, she told the dealer that she could not allow anything to be sold because the sculptures all fitted into her luxurious suburban home so well that she could not live without them. One can understand the doubts raised by my "misogynist" dealer friend! It had never occurred to this woman's dealer to require a written statement that he could sell the sculpture. Perhaps he should have, for I have heard a number of artists say, "I am not particularly interested in sales; I just want to have a one-man show and establish a professional reputation." It is a good idea to remember that galleries are "dealing"; they must make a living; they are not in business merely for the artist's own prestige. Dealers, in short, cannot be purely esthetic philanthropists.

A well-known, seasoned artist who had an exclusive contract with an established gallery was invited not long ago to join another, larger gallery in the middle of his contract year. Although he had been around long enough to know better, he blithely accepted the new offer and was chagrined to find that he had to face a law suit, which he quite rightly lost.

Media, special problems

If you work primarily on paper—watercolors, drawings, prints—you should be prepared to realize that the more "expensive" galleries will probably feel that they cannot afford to handle your output. For "papers" usually bring lower prices than canvases or sculptures. Dealers with high overhead costs need to hang higher priced work on their walls, relegating the artist's papers to portfolios in the back room for those customers who say, "I like this artist's work, but haven't you something less costly?"

This fact does not mean that your papers will not find a market; it means, rather, that you are more likely to find your market in galleries located where rents are lower than in the major art section of a city, or else in the suburbs.

Artists who straddle the art-craft fields still have some difficulty in finding outlets, but this situation is gradually being eased. A bronze pot may well be a work of sculpture; a stained-glass panel or a tapestry may be as fully a work of fine art as a painting. But the tendency has been to classify such works as craft rather than art, simply because of their form or medium. Their outlets have been limited to America House (operated in New York under the Craftsmen's Council), or to certain art-craft gift shops and showrooms. Fine arts galleries and museums are beginning to recognize these art-craft expressions.

This change in attitude has been given a shot in the arm by developments such as the collection of three hundred contemporary "art-objects" formed by the Johnson Wax Company for international circulation and subsequent donation to the Smithsonian Institution in Washington. Art-craft objects have also received a boost from the impressive series of exhibitions developed in recent seasons by New York's Museum of Contemporary Crafts. An unusual store on First Avenue between 63rd and 64th Streets opened in New York in 1968 for "art as objects," serving as an outlet for new forms of art. It seems probable that the craft-as-art movement will spread to more museums, galleries, and stores.

Precision in inquiries

If artists and dealers are considered vague, temperamental, and imprecise, certain would-be purchasers can top them any day. How would you answer a note like the one that arrived at the Art Information Center, sent from Connecticut?: "My husband and I are interested in buying an oil painting. We would like something large, approximately 24" x 36", or 30" x 40", and hope to find one in a semi-abstract or impressionist style at a moderate cost." Or an inquiry from an Arizona motel?: "We would like very much to get information and brochures on large steel figures, true form rather than geometric. We have in mind objects that are over ten feet high."

The inexplicit aspect becomes much more incredible when a professional in the field, the art director of a mid-western institution, can write with such imprecision: "We intend to present a major Art Gallery, in which we hope to display the finest art works available. I hope you will send me whatever information you can provide on the many aspects of Contemporary Art. Our gallery intends to exhibit the finest Art of a local, national, international nature and I eagerly await your reply." Even the Queens housewife contemplating her first art purchase was much more direct and to the point. Should she buy "a beautiful hand-painted head of a gypsy, all framed, for $75? I like it," she said, "but I want to know whether it will increase in value in a couple of years."

Whether you request information from the Art Information Center, from a gallery or museum, from a foundation, or whatever, you can expect a sensible, informative reply only if you state your queries in a specific and sensible way. Know exactly what you want; ask for it simply and clearly. You'll be gratified by the response.

Appendix

Contract form

Many galleries draw up some kind of a contract which artist and dealer sign before holding a one-man show. These contracts vary considerably; sometimes they are not a form at all, but merely an exchange of letters; occasionally, agreements are purely verbal. The following, filled out in duplicate, is a typical formal contract.

1. The (name) .... Gallery, (address) ...., referred to hereafter as the "Gallery" agrees to act as sales representative for (artist's name) ...., referred to hereafter as the "Artist," for a period of .... year(s) from date.

2. The Gallery shall receive ....%, [33⅓% in many places, 40% in New York and other large art centers] of all sales made on its premises.

3. The Gallery shall receive ....% of all portrait, sculpture or mural commissions that it gets for the Artist, and ....% of any others awarded during the contract period [because the gallery's promotion has built the artist's reputation; and because the artist may not sell directly in competition with his dealer].

4. The Gallery shall not receive any commissions on royalties, sale of reproduction rights, or commercial assignments unless arranged by the Gallery, in which case the commission will be ....%. It shall be understood that all sales are

made exclusive of reproduction rights, and written acknowledgment of that fact shall be obtained from purchaser by the Gallery. Reproduction rights may be specifically purchased with the Artist's written consent in each case.

5. The Gallery shall not receive commissions on prizes or awards granted to the Artist by art institutions, foundations, or a government agency.

6. During the period of the contract, the Artist shall not contract for any other representation, except in the following fields if they do not conflict with the Gallery's outlets:
   a. representation outside the city in which the Gallery is located
   b. foreign countries
   c. multiples

The Gallery may arrange for representation of the Artist by another agency, but will pay such agency by splitting its own commission.

7. The Gallery will act as continuous sales representative for the Artist, keeping always available a few examples of work. The Gallery will exhibit the work of the Artist in a one-man show of .... weeks' duration [usually just under three weeks]. At least one work will be exhibited in all gallery group shows.

8. The costs of a one-man show will be borne by the Gallery, except for publicity costs, the actual bills for which are to be paid by the Artist. Publicity costs will be deemed to include only the costs of: printing and mailing of brochure; advertisements; photographs for the press; preview costs (if any). The Artist agrees to pay publicity costs in advance.

9. The Gallery will pay costs of packing and shipping work sent to clients and exhibitions. It will insure work against loss or damage while the work is on its premises only; insurance will be at .... % [average: 40%–60%] of price the Artist would receive if the work were sold.

10. A written agreement will be signed by Artist and Gallery on prices for all work left on consignment. Only with the written consent of the Artist may the Gallery accept a lower price. Should the Gallery obtain a higher price, it is guaranteed that the Artist will receive his same percentage of the total proceeds.

11. Payment to the Artist for any sales made by the Gallery shall be made within fifteen days from the date payment is received. If payment is to be made in installments, the Artist's prior consent shall be required, and payment to the Artist shall be made within fifteen days after final payment is received.

12. All works are received by the Gallery on consignment and in trust. The net proceeds of all sums received by the Gallery on account of works sold shall, after deduction of commission and expenses agreed upon, belong to the Artist.

13. The Gallery will give the Artist a written receipt for all work received; the Artist will sign a receipt for all work returned.

14. The Gallery shall keep records of transactions regarding each Artist's work, records which the Artist may inspect at any time during business hours.

15. This agreement may be canceled by either party up to three months prior to the opening of a one-man show by giving five days' written notice. No cancellation may become effective, however, if the printing or advertising for a show has already been placed.

Date: . . . .

Gallery Official . . . .

Artist . . . .

Bill of Sale Form   (*to be filled out in duplicate*)

Place ....

Date ....

Name ....

Address ....

Sold to: ....

Description of work: Price:

Terms of payment:

Reproduction rights reserved

Purchaser (Signed) ....

Authorized Dealer or Artist ....

Receipt Form   (*to be filled out in duplicate*)

Received from:

Name of Artist ....

Address ....

Phone ....

Title	Medium	Size	Sales Price	% Commission
1.				
2.				
3.				

To be held until (date) ....

While the works listed above are on the Gallery's premises, they will be insured against loss or damage for the benefit of the Artist at   % of the sales price less commission. None may be removed during the exhibition except as agreed in writing. Reproduction rights reserved by the Artist.

Date ....

Authorized Dealer ....

Artists' Equity Association, Inc.

Described as a National Organization for Professional Fine Artists, Artists' Equity's National ·Headquarters is at 229 Broadway East, Seattle, Washington 98102.

Artists' Equity Assn. of New York, Inc. is a separate unit, not affiliated with the National. It has its own offices and exhibition space at 1780 Broadway (57th Street), New York, N.Y. 10019. As of 1969, the President is Mr. Hy Cohen.

Elsewhere in the country there are seventeen chapters— which are affiliated with the National—as follows:

National Officers and Board of Directors as of June 1969

President:

LaVerne Krause, 3295 W. 16th, Eugene, Oregon 97402.

Secretary-Treasurer:

William Hixson, 4220 E. 90th, Seattle, Wash. 98115.

Chapter Presidents: (Members of the Board)

ALBUQUERQUE: Walter Bambrook, 1717 Bryn Mawr, N.E., Albuquerque, N.M. 87104.

BOULDER: Gwendolyn Meux, 1520 Baseline, Boulder, Colo.

CENTRAL AREA: Robert Shuler, 7123 Franklin, Des Moines, Iowa.

CHICAGO: Tim Meier, 2514 Pioneer Rd., Evanston, Ill. 60201.

DENVER: Ed Towbin, 1820 Bellaire, Denver, Colo. 80220.

FLORIDA: Reyna Youngerman, 3000 Prairie Ave., Miami Beach, Fla. 33140.

MARYLAND: Marie Larsen, 311 Dunkirk Rd., Baltimore, Md. 21212.

MINNESOTA: Robert Burg, 1318 W. Maynard Dr., St. Paul, Minn. 55116.

NEW ENGLAND: Garabed Der Hohanessian, 52 Angell St., Providence, R.I. 02906.

NORTHERN CALIFORNIA: Robert Kingsbury, 760 Wisconsin St., San Francisco, Calif. 94107.

OREGON: Roger Long, 443 7th, Lake Oswego, Oregon 97034.

PHILADELPHIA: Libby Newman, 327 Meeting House Lane, Merion Station, Pa. 19066.

SANTA FÉ: Helen Rumpel, 320 Cadiz Rd., Santa Fé, N.M. 87501.

ST. LOUIS: Phyllis Margolin, 24 Ladue Manor, St. Louis 24, Mo.

SOUTHERN CALIFORNIA: Charles Mattox, 326 B Market St., Venice, Calif. 90291.

WASHINGTON, D.C.: Marcella Comes, 3106 P St., N.W., Washington, D.C. 20007.

WASHINGTON STATE: Victoria Savage, 20309 8th Ave. N.W. Seattle, Wash. 98177.

National Vice Presidents:

Una Hansbury, 5035 Eskridge Terrace N.W., Washington, D.C. 20016.

Joseph Greenberg, Jr., 1629 Ludlow St., Philadelphia, Pa. 19103.

Walter Bambrook, 1717 Bryn Mawr N.E., Albuquerque, N.M. 87104.

Julia Pearl, 351 Madrone Park Circle, Mill Valley, Calif. 94941.

L. A. D. Montgomery, 413 Church Road, Philadelphia, Pa. 19111.

Warning to artists, dealers, and collectors in the field of prints

Fraud and misrepresentation, particularly in the field of printmaking, have been all too common over the years. The word *print* is an unfortunately ambiguous term: it *does* mean a work of fine art; but it also means a photograph, a color reproduction, a designed cloth or fabric (as in a "print dress"), and even a "print of butter" made from a mold. The semantic latitude of the word *print* has made it easier for the unscrupulous to cash in on the market eager to buy genuine original prints as works of art. The public, often insufficiently informed as to what constitutes an "original print," is therefore easily fooled. What we really need is a new word to convey a rigid concept of an original print (Noah Webster would undoubtedly turn over in his grave, so we are probably stuck with the word we have).

The Print Council of America

The Print Council of America, whose directors include major United States experts in the field, has made valiant efforts to stem the tide of these fraudulent practices. You can get their valuable pamphlet, "What Is an Original Print?", which gives some historical background of print-making, outlines processes and techniques, and offers definitions and distinctions between original and counterfeit prints (The Print Council of America, 527 Madison Ave., New York, N.Y. 10022; 50 cents).

The Council has perpetuated a legal definition now accepted by the U.S. Customs, by the French *Chambre Syndicat de l'Estampe,* and by the International Association of Plastic Arts of UNESCO. It reads as follows:

"An original print is a work of art, the general requirements of which are:

1. The artist alone has created the master image in or upon the plate, stone, woodblock, or other material for the purpose of creating the print.

2. The print is made from the said material by the artist or pursuant to his directions.

3. The finished print is approved by the artist."

Although the Council's aims and definitions are directed primarily to the layman and collector "as a protection against deceptive fraud," they are surely of equal, if not greater, concern to the artist and the dealer. Because of the sharp practices that have developed in the field, artists and dealers may often be just as much in need of definitions to avoid falling inadvertently into the trap.

The legal definition just stated does not preclude the possibility of teamwork between artist and master printer, which is inherent in the wording ". . . made by the artist *or pursuant to his directions,*" and "The finished print is *approved* by the artist" (italics mine). Collaboration by artists and highly skilled printers, which goes back to the practices of many old masters, has recently experienced a revival, one partly due to the 11-year (1959-70) operation of the Los Angeles Tamarind Lithography Workshop, sponsored by the Ford Foundation. There is no particular reason why a fine artist should take the time to inform himself on the intricate printing techniques so well known to the master printer, as long as the artist-creator is the final arbiter of the product. The relationship is somewhat similar to that between a sculptor and his bronze-caster.

But it has been too easy for everyone—artist, dealer, and collector—to be duped by excellent reproductions, produced either photomechanically in unlimited editions (as in some of the so-called "original" Toulouse-Lautrec posters); or made by craftsmen as copy-reproductions, often in limited editions and even signed and numbered by the artists (these are nevertheless definitely not "originals"). Only by a thorough knowledge of the distinctions that make a truly "original" print can the artist and dealer—as well as the collector—be sure to avoid participating in practices that are considered fraudulent. Awareness of these distinctions is becoming more and more widespread; with it public sentiment against malpractices is becoming more aroused. Those who indulge in malpractices, therefore, will only find their reputation and stature diminished as a result.

New York State laws affecting the fine arts

The following are summaries of some recently enacted New York State laws specifically related to the field of fine arts (paintings, sculpture, drawings, and works of graphic art). Their concepts are generally more advanced than legislation in other parts of the country. It is therefore to be hoped that they will set precedents. Art organizations desiring to promote such laws in their own states may obtain the full texts from: Office of the Attorney General, State Office Building, 80 Centre Street, New York, N.Y. 10013.

Reproduction rights

(Chapter 668, L. 1966. Gen. Bus. Law Article 12-E). This law requires that whenever a work of fine art is sold by the artist or his agent, the "right of reproduction" is retained by the artist unless he expressly transfers it in writing (usually for a fee) to the purchaser. Formerly their right of reproduction automatically passed to the purchaser with the transfer of the physical object. The "right of reproduction" is defined as including prints suitable for framing, facsimile casts of sculpture, greeting cards, reproductions in general books, magazines, and sections of newspapers not devoted primarily to art (when the reproductions are used for purposes for which publishers customarily pay), art films, television (except educational programs), and any form of advertising. The "right of reproduction" does *not* include museum publications of exhibition catalogs, books, slides, photographs, postcards, and other small prints not suitable for framing; reproductions in art publications, in educational books and magazines (where the reproductions are not used for purposes for which publishers customarily pay), on slides and film strips not intended for a mass audience.

Artist-dealer relationships

(Chapter 984, L. 1966, as amended by Chapter 454 L. 1968; Gen. Bus. Law Article 12-C). When an artist delivers his work to a dealer who accepts it for sale on a commission basis, the work is deemed, under this law, to be "on consignment" (the artist retaining ownership), and the dealer is deemed to be the artist's agent. The dealer may not wrongfully withhold or appropriate for his own use any such works of art or the proceeds of sale thereof, or he may be subject to prosecution for larceny under the Penal Law. Any contract or agreement which calls for waiving these provisions is absolutely void, except that an artist may voluntarily sign a written waiver with respect only to the proceeds of sales in the hands of a dealer over and above the first $2,500 gross in any twelve-month period.

The Attorney General's Office stated, after a lengthy and intensive investigation, that many artists had difficulty in recovering their works after an exhibition and in obtaining their proceeds from works sold by their dealers. This situation is made more acute by the fact that of New York City's some 400 galleries, about 10% go out of business each year. As stated by Hy Cohen, President of Artists' Equity of New York, in support of the Attorney General's legislation: "Many of the new galleries which appear on the art scene each year hope to cash in on the current expanded interest in the collecting of works of art. Most of these are 'shoestring' galleries operating largely on the artist's share of proceeds of sales without investing a nickel of their own money. . . . If artists' funds were treated as 'trust' funds right from the start the art business might perhaps become less attractive to a certain undesirable element, but at least the artist would not be quite as helpless in dealing with this element."

Seizure of work

An Act (Chapter 1065, L. 1968, Gen. Bus. Law Article 12-G) to exempt from seizure works of fine art of non-residents while on exhibition for cultural or other non-profit purposes. This law provides that no process of any kind of seizure shall be levied on any work of fine art while en route to or from, or while on exhibition or deposited by a non-resident exhibitor for exhibition at a museum, university or other non-profit organization for educational, charitable or other purposes not for profit to the exhibitor. The new law protects a non-resident art lender from any harassment or impounding of his art by local creditors or sheriffs. Thus lenders—whether public collections, private collectors, or artists, from all over the United States and abroad—are encouraged to enhance cultural exhibitions held in New York. The law does not affect the rights of creditors of non-residents whose works are sent to New York for sale purposes.

Liability for counterfeits

Another recent New York State law, recommended by New York State Attorney General Louis J. Lefkowitz, makes art dealers, auctioneers and their consignors legally liable, despite an express disclaimer, if a work of fine art purchased by a "non-merchant" turns out to be a counterfeit or a mis-attribution (Gen. Bus. Law Article 12-D).

Gen. Bus. Law Article 12-F makes it a Class A misdemeanor for an art expert knowingly to authenticate a counterfeit work of art with intent to defraud. A Class A misdemeanor is punishable by a $1,000 fine, a year in prison, or both. The Attorney General had found that art swindles were easier to perpetrate if the seller was armed with a certificate of authenticity by a recognized expert.

Index

Edited by Judith A. Levy

Designed by James Craig

Composed in twelve point Caledonia by Nashville Composition, Inc.

Printed and bound by Halliday Lithograph Corporation